Praise for *Plan BE*

"This book is a gem! It provides an intuitive model for success which allows us to heal, tap into our wisdom, connect deeply with ourselves and others, and gives us the courage and the strength to show up authentically."

Christel Reynaerts, former CEO, BMW Financial Services Belgium and CEO Alphabet Netherlands and Belgium

"At a time when so many of our systems are in need of deep, far-reaching reform, Peter reminds us that all systems and organizational change starts with human change. Plan BE is a rallying cry for personal authenticity and a pathway to true success."

Paul Polman, business leader, co-author of *Net Positive: How Courageous Companies Thrive By Giving More Than They Take*

"Plan BE is an exceptional book that reveals a path to transport you from wherever you may be, to BE the best of you. It outlines a New Operating System for life – aligning your life with your purpose and inner calling, being fully present in each living moment. An amazing book, based on the author's lifelong reflections and his passion to make every individual achieve their highest potential, while making it naturally easy to lead with authenticity, and live with a sense of perpetual satisfaction and fulfillment."

Ravi Chaudhry, former chairman Tata Group Companies. Author of *Quest for Exceptional Leadership: Mirage to Reality*

"The new model of success is the gateway to possibility. I am filled with gratitude for being exposed to *Plan BE* and its concepts. This book gives me the tools to a life of abundance that is intended for us all."

Diane Carazas, Executive Board Member and
Regional Director Latin America, CARE

"I have witnessed myself the outstanding results the *Plan BE* model can bring in a global corporation, enjoying the sense of flow and creating an environment where people enjoy working together in an authentic and trustful environment. Engagement, collaboration, creativity, innovation, and ultimate financial success happen flawlessly."

Carlos Sarmiento, Director Diversity and Inclusion, SLB

"The simple, yet powerful concepts Peter brings forth in Plan BE provide the wisdom needed in this exact point in time to help individuals recognize that we hold the power to transform ourselves, our families, our businesses and communities to confidently tackle the complex challenges in our daily lives. As a global business leader and certified executive coach, I often searched for ways to expand individual coaching concepts beyond the individual to resonate with teams and organizations. After adopting Peter's concepts and witnessing the ensuing transformation they brought, I believe passionately that by embracing these concepts in all areas of life it is possible to transcend the perceived boundaries of all relationships. Peter has a magical yet practical way of delivering the concepts in this book."

Paty Shives, global HR leader and executive coach

"If you've ever felt exhausted, overwhelmed, and stressed, and wondered if there's more to life than the repetitive hamster wheel... this book has a powerful and refreshing new look at how we can change that! This book has changed my life. I strongly encourage you to read every page of this book. Peter Matthies provides an important map to guide us into and through these timely and necessary changes in our world."

Pamala Oslie, best-selling author of *Life Colors,*
Infinite You, and Make Your Dreams Come True

"Plan BE is a groundbreaking book that takes us on a transformative journey towards a new paradigm of success. In a world where the traditional approach often leads to exhaustion and burnout, Plan BE offers an alternative pathway that allows individuals to thrive and flourish while staying true to their authentic selves. Plan BE is not simply a how-to book; it is a revelation that opens up a room of satisfaction, inner power, and a solution that many of us have sensed but struggled to access. With its profound insights and practical guidance, Plan BE paves the way for a more fulfilling and purposeful life, both individually and collectively. It is a must-read for anyone seeking a new way of approaching success and unlocking their full potential."

Johannes May, CEO, Swiss Property AG

"The phrase 'you are not a human doing but a human being' woke me up. The discussions I had with Peter, and the concept that now is key of this book, reminded me not working in actionism but instead reconnecting me to a greater good of my job. I refocused on my strengths, remembered who I am and the higher purpose I was striving for when I took on my leadership role. The new success model in this book puts it into a simple formula."

Dr. Mirjam Storim, Head of Innovation Strategy
and Strategic Value Creation, BMW Group

"Many of us have realized that our current success model has become a recipe for failure, but few know how to change it. Peter Matthies is one of the few. In Plan BE, he has finally decided to share his secrets. This book is a rare gift because it demonstrates how to claim your authentic power and identify the hidden mechanisms of your subconscious programming that hold you back from living a wholesome life, both privately and professionally. A must read."

Dr. Mariana Bozesan, Europe's Female Investor 2019, Member Club of Rome, Fellow World Academy of Art and Science, and author of *Integral Investing*

"Plan BE offers big and practical solutions to bring balance to everyday work life challenges. Peter Matthies shares years of his own personal experiences, research and on the ground training to make accessible what otherwise can remain hidden until a crisis strikes. I highly recommend this book as a guide to the future. Searching for purpose, meaning or true wealth? Plan BE delivers a pathway to your health, happiness and inner peace. Peter Matthies is a business Sage that can save you from endlessly searching to discover your true calling. This book could very well save you lifetimes of struggles and inner loneliness. If you read one book in the coming year, make sure it's Plan BE!

Adam C Hall, author of *The Divine Genius, Earthkeeper* and *Abundance and Miracles*. CEO of the Genius Studio

"In this new era in which vibration, sound and light are producing new ways of being, we human beings have the potential to actualize a new way of being for ourselves collectively and each of us individually. This book invites you to embark on a new kind of journey; a way to actualize your Authentic Self. A new way of being consistent with the vibration that you are."

Bill Sechrest, attorney, entrepreneur, author

Plan BE

A Professional's Guide
to Authentic Success

PETER MATTHIES

CONSCIOUS
BUSINESS INSTITUTE
PUBLISHING

Published by Conscious Business Institute Publishing®, Santa Barbara, CA and by
Best Seller Publishing®
Conscious Business Institute Publishing® and Best Seller Publishing ®
are registered trademarks.
Printed in the United States of America.

ISBN: 979-8-218-28444-2

This publication is designed to provide accurate and authoritative information with regard to the subject matter covered. It is sold with the understanding that the publisher is not engaged in rendering legal, accounting, or other professional advice. If legal advice or other expert assistance is required, the services of a competent professional should be sought. The opinions expressed by the author in this book are not endorsed by Best Seller Publishing® and are the sole responsibility of the author rendering the opinion.

For more information, please write:
Conscious Business Institute Publishing
424 E Micheltorena St.
Santa Barbara, CA 93101
or call +1 (866) 449-3720
Visit us online at: www.ConsciousBusinessInstitute.com

To Rosalina,
for always encouraging me to live my authenticity.

CONTENTS

INTRODUCTION

Our present model for success is broken. We know it's broken because even when we get ahead in life, make a lot of money, and reach a good position, the majority of us are still left with the deep-seated feeling that something important is missing. When we put our head on the pillow at night we think, *There's got to be more to life. Is this really all there is?* Juggling the daily pressures and expectations, more and more people are stressed out, missing fulfillment, wondering if there's an alternative – a better way to work and succeed in life.

This pervasive yearning to succeed without depleting our life energy in the corporate hamster wheel is a fundamental problem in our culture. With more than 40 percent of all illnesses related to workplace stress, this problem causes suffering for millions of people. But this steady background noise of questioning and longing doesn't just cause pain in our personal lives, it undermines the effectiveness and goals of every organization. It reveals a fundamental flaw in the way we run our businesses: most of today's companies are unable to truly engage their employees and fulfill their deeper needs. As a result, more than three-quarters of our workforce are disengaged, unsatisfied, and ready to quit – if they just knew how to make money in a more inspiring or fun way.

This book provides a new success model, for you individually and for your organization. It provides a new framework — a new operating system for personal and business success. However, this is not a how-to book. You've probably read many how-to books and realized, although they might provide good tips, they haven't made your life much easier. This book reveals the fundamental dynamics and perceptions, the invisible forces that shape our lives. It provides insight into the hidden patterns of our decisions and conditioning, creating a consciousness change that will have a ripple effect into every part of your life: your personal relationships, your career, your business, and your physical health and well-being.

Even if you feel that your life is working well, this book will make you aware of how your current success model works, the symptoms it creates, and its effect on our world at large. Only then can we find a cure to the increasing challenges in our world and address them at their source: the way we decide.

The first time I was hit with the feelings of emptiness and dissatisfaction at work was during grad school. During the semester breaks, I worked at Siemens' largest research facility just outside Munich. We called the place "Lego Land" because the large buildings looked as though they were pieced together with gigantic red, blue, and white Lego cubes. Like any high-tech research facility, Lego Land was protected by tall, sturdy metal fences. Every morning, 12,000 Siemens employees passed through heavy, revolving iron gates to get to work. Many times, I stepped away from the flow of the masses to watch the hordes of people enter the "Iron Gates." Every time, I was shocked to see that most of them — from engineer to executive — seemed to check out of their "real life" the moment the big iron gates turned. As though an invisible force sucked part of their spirit out of them the moment they realized it would be *just another day at work.*

A few weeks later I became one of them. Every morning, I sat in the subway, my body swaying to the rhythm of the train tracks, comfortably numb, reading the daily paper. And when it was my time to turn the heavy iron doors, a part of my life force, my passion, and my energy was sucked out of me too.

Lunchtime was the highlight of my day. With a small group of peers, I would walk through endless corridors to reach the cafeteria. After lunch, weather permitting, we took a short stroll through the artificially landscaped areas. And then back to our desks in faraway corners of the Lego cubes. At the end of the day, when it was time to go home and I turned the big iron gates again, I felt empty and sad – too tired to check back into my "real life." As the weeks passed, it became clear that this way of working turned us into machines, without the possibility to express our true personality, unique essence, and distinctive abilities. And although my success grew over time, I didn't know that this sobering experience by the iron gates would become a steadfast companion for many years of my career.

Years later, when I worked for Accenture on a client assignment in the Netherlands, I woke up in my hotel room on a rainy morning – struck with the same feeling I had when I watched the masses of people pass through Siemens' iron gates. After I walked into the bathroom and looked at myself in the mirror, a series of questions surfaced from a deep place within me I couldn't yet recognize: *Is this what you want to be doing? You have a great job. Why don't you feel happy and alive?* When I spoke with some friends at the company, I realized I wasn't the only one asking these questions. As it turned out, many of my colleagues shared the same pressing concerns: virtually everyone agreed that the feeling our culture promised "success" would bring, never came.

By the time I was running a software startup in Germany, the constant pressure and questioning brought me to a crossroads. Early one evening, I was so immersed in working on a computer system that I completely forgot the world around me. The nagging question of why these darn computers always have to break took up most of my brain power, not leaving much attention for anything else. When I looked up at last, I saw the sun setting, casting its last rays in a stunning alpenglow across the Zugspitze, Germany's highest mountain, and the rest of the Alps. The soft red light was so present, so timeless, and so powerful, it seemed as though the world had come to a standstill. It was a moment of complete stillness and beauty – until, from that stillness, those familiar questions bubbled to the surface again: *What am I doing here? What's the purpose of all this? Is this what I'm supposed to be doing with my life?*

With those questions filling my mind, I decided there and then I had to find an answer. While quitting my job or completely leaving the rat race behind me had crossed my mind, I knew this wasn't the solution. Like most of us, I wanted to accomplish something in my life, to make a difference. I realized I was searching for a better way to succeed – a career that fulfilled me without constantly having to work harder to get ahead. I was looking for a way to build businesses where people wouldn't just bring their bodies and minds to work but also their hearts and souls. Was that too much to ask?

A Silent Crisis

Later, as a venture capitalist, I discovered how pervasive this problem is; even wealthy managers who had *made it* asked the same questions and had the same longings. My job as a venture investor was to find the most promising startups and assess their management teams. We funneled ten, twenty, sometimes fifty executives through our meeting rooms each day – all of them pitching to get a big investment for their companies.

They had ambition, they pushed their business ahead, and many of them had tired eyes. Listening to countless presentations over the years, I started wondering what these executives were really thinking, what they *really* wanted beyond our investment or their businesses hitting the top of the charts.

After interviewing hundreds of executives, I was shocked to find that only five to ten percent of them were truly fulfilled and satisfied. With a little probing, I discovered most of these top-notch, accomplished managers were challenged with the same stress, exhaustion, or lack of fulfillment almost all of us complain about. While the lucky five to ten percent seemed like fish in water – happy with their work and usually quite successful – the other 90 percent were struggling with money or time (often both), a clear indication that something wasn't right. Many of them were unhappy, distanced from their spouses or children, filling the void with work, possessions, exercise, or affairs. Others were using alcohol and drugs, prescribed or not, as a relief from the pressure, worries, and lack of emotional fulfillment.

Greg, an executive at a large telecommunications company, confessed to me: "If I'm being honest, I'm spinning my wheels. I'm supposed to help lead the business, but all I do is cater to a boss with a big ego. He seems to rule the entire business. I feel burnt out, exhausted – there's always more to do. When I get home, my wife and children demand my time. It's just continuous. There's no space, no time for myself. I am making good money, but honestly, it feels as though I am just wasting my life."

At first, I wondered whether the challenges people face are stronger in certain companies or geographic areas and less pervasive in others. After working with executives and businesses from the Americas, Europe, and Asia for more than 20 years, I found these problems are not only universal, but also drastically increasing with the accelerating change, complexity, and pace of the business world. As more people told me their stories, forgetting their titles or agendas, they revealed what was really going on inside of them.

"I am making $600,000 per year in my business. I have a great house, my children are in good schools, and I'm getting stellar feedback from my clients. But my life feels empty. The relationship with my wife is dead, and I don't know how I can bring that back to life. Is all the business success worth it?"

"I'm a director in a Fortune 100 corporation. I have wanted to reach this position since my late teens. Now, I start work at seven in the morning and get home just before my children go to bed. I need the weekends to recover, but it's the only time I have with my kids. And every year, our board is increasing the pressure – demanding to cut costs by another 20 percent."

"I'm the founder of a successful startup. I should be very happy because I have my own business. But I'm always second-guessing myself: *What else could I do? What can I do better? Am I doing the right thing to grow my company?* There's always this pressure and anxiety, and it takes away my joy in life. What I'd really love to do is open a small restaurant with delicious food and a family atmosphere in southern France."

"I work as an anchor at a large media conglomerate. It is a great job, but for some reason I have lost my passion and zest for life. What do I really want to do? I dream about refurbishing and running a small hotel that I saw on this beautiful, remote beach in Kenya."

These painful problems never make the headlines. Yet they're far-reaching and fundamental problems in our society, causing quiet suffering for millions of people. This deep-seated dissatisfaction doesn't just create pain in our personal lives. It reveals a fundamental flaw in the way we conduct business – that most of today's businesses are unable to fulfill the deeper needs, desires, and values we hold as individuals.

As a venture capitalist, these declarations made me hold my breath because they brought up fundamental questions about how effectively we put our money to work: If our firm decided to invest $10 to $20 million in a startup or even larger chunks of $50 to $100 million when acquiring entire organizations such as Tommy Hilfiger, Calvin Klein, or the British Yellow Pages, how effective was our investment if only a fraction of the team was fully on board? How many millions did we lose because people's minds and hearts were focused on a beach in Kenya or their dispute with some guy in finance rather than on building an exceptional organization?

Our Model of Success: A Recipe for Frustration

After observing this problem over and over again – and after feeling the growing pressure in my own life – I finally decided that I had to change something. My body was exhausted from working 13 to 15 hours every day, feeling guilty when I left the office on Fridays before six at night. At first, I took a few clumsy attempts to breathe some soul into my life by going on weekend skiing trips, attending yoga classes, and scheduling drumming lessons; but I had arrived at a point where beating on some congas, doing sun salutations, or breathing the crisp mountain air couldn't change my everyday mood anymore. Two friends with equally "successful" careers joined me for the weekly drumming classes, and there we sat in a circle in a dark jazz club, in dark suits and white shirts, pounding away on the congas like a flock of depressed penguins.

One winter evening, returning home from another long workday, my wife asked whether I wanted to go out for dinner or watch a movie.

During prior months, my usual answer had become "either way is fine." But this evening, hearing my answer shocked me to my bones. I realized that I wasn't "fine either way." I couldn't make a decision. I had become so cut off from my feelings that I simply didn't know what I wanted anymore. I had become like Marvin, the robot from *The Hitchhiker's Guide to the Galaxy* who is afflicted with chronic depression and gloominess. How could I ever feel alive and fulfilled if I was so numb inside that I couldn't even decide whether I wanted to eat or watch a movie?

The more I thought about my sobering discovery, the clearer it became: if I wanted to find a different way to work and succeed in my life, not just reduce the hours I spent at work or find more balance, but to truly live with well-being, purpose, and success, I had to quit "the system."

As Albert Einstein said, "Problems cannot be solved with the same level of thinking that created them." And so, with Einstein's wind at my back, I decided to leave. I left the venture capital business. I left my home country. I left my friends. I even left my flailing marriage. Two suitcases in hand, I moved to California. I felt great. With enough money for a couple of years, I was ready to press the reset button and build a new career. I had decided to turn my life into an experiment: to "burn my boats" to my old work-life and develop a new approach for business – one that's not only financially successful but also allows people to grow into their authenticity.

I loved the freshness, the freedom, the possibilities; at the same time, I grew anxious about the tremendous uncertainties of my endeavor. After only a few months, I began oscillating between happiness and anxiety, wondering whether my decision had been courageous or plain foolish. A very fine line, I noted. How would I earn money? I wanted a new career, but what on earth would that look like? It turned out that I didn't have to answer these questions yet. After only six months,

I noticed I had regretfully recreated the same life as before. I had switched continents, people, and careers, and yet I repeated the same sense of overwork, pressure, and worries from my "old life." I realized, after years of beating around the bush and changing outside circumstances, I had to go to *the source*.

In the following years, I searched for and met with hundreds of people throughout the Americas, Europe, and Asia – individuals who appeared to have bridged financial success with a sense of purpose and fulfillment in their lives: successful entrepreneurs and businesspeople, well-known artists, medical professionals, research scholars, even psychics and healers who lived off the beaten track of society. I spent weeks at a time with indigenous cultures – Native American medicine people, Peruvian shamans, and Hawaiian kahunas – and compared their way of life, their behaviors and thinking, with the Western approach to life. The further I went down the rabbit hole, the more I discovered that the root of our problems and struggles point to a single source: our current model of success.

I realized it is not just conventional wisdom that prompts us to *work harder* and *do more* to get ahead in life. Consciously or unconsciously, we follow a specific model of success that is amazingly universal for anyone growing up in the "developed world." It is this model of success that's making us suffer. In fact, our common model of success isn't *designed* to make us happy. And it is also the cause for most of the world's suffering – from families fighting over who's getting the silver to countries fighting over power or natural resources.

More than a decade of questioning and research took me to the core dysfunction of this model, uncovering what I call the governing principle of "Dominance & Subservience." This principle of thinking is so deeply ingrained in our culture and our daily lives that it unknowingly determines many of our behaviors and decisions, which ultimately causes the stress, struggle, and conflict we experience in our day-to-day lives. This governing principle is the reason that – even if we change jobs, relationships, or the country we live in – we tend to recreate similar experiences: success in some areas and struggle in others. Over and over. In both our personal lives and businesses, the Model of Dominance & Subservience operates like a malfunctioning compass, taking us not closer but farther away from the things we truly desire.

At times I believed there were no alternatives to this governing principle – that we're stuck with our present model of success, that this is the only way to get ahead in life. But part of me was convinced there was a better way. A subtle voice kept reminding me: *You don't have to live your life like this. Keep looking.* There *is* a model of true success – a *Plan B* – that allows us to prosper financially as we expand into our full authenticity, to create deep and meaningful connections with the people around us, and to contribute to a bigger purpose so we can ultimately know: This is it. *This* is the life I am meant to live.

Our Common Journey

As I ventured out to find a better model, it became clear that I wasn't only finding a solution for our personal struggles but also a solution to a much broader problem in our society, a *systemic* issue that impacts the way we live our lives, relate to each other, lead our businesses, and even build our governments. In fact, I've realized that our existing model of success lies at the core of the deepest, most widespread problems in our world. Most of us, in our quiet moments, know this is true.

We're standing at a crossroads, both as individuals and as a society. Our future will be defined by the success model we ultimately choose to follow. If we continue to pursue success, make money, build our careers, and lead our corporations with the existing Model of Dominance & Subservience, where getting ahead means we need to do more, work harder, and control outcomes, we'll find ourselves even more frustrated, exhausted, or unfulfilled in our work, and our natural environment even more depleted.

We need to change the existing model in an attempt to cope with the growing demands and challenges in our daily lives. We need a different path – one that doesn't just deliver the personal fulfillment, satisfaction, peace of mind, and financial rewards that we all desire, but one that can also help us create more effective organizations, more spiritually fulfilling connections with each other, and a lifestyle that sustains our planet.

This book is about an alternative pathway to success – a new paradigm that doesn't require you to exhaust yourself to get ahead but instead allows you to expand into the unique personality you're here to *Be*.

To get there, part one will walk you through the far-reaching impact of our current model of success: from individual struggle and organizational breakdowns to political conflicts and the destruction of our natural environment. You'll be introduced to an alternative model for success that enables you to break away from business as usual and create success by swimming downstream rather than upstream.

As you start implementing the new success model in your life, you'll learn about your authenticity – who you're here to *Be* during this lifetime. I'll introduce you to your unique Magic, that unique contribution you're here to bring into the world where work becomes a flow. You'll discover your purpose and those deep personal drivers, which provide you with energy and direction. As you expand into your authentic power, you'll learn about the hidden mechanism – the subconscious programming that holds you back. You'll understand why we create stress and struggle in our lives and how you can rewrite your inner programming.

In part two, you'll apply the new success model to your broader life. First, to create more fulfilling and life-giving relationships and then to create a work environment that aligns with your authentic personality. Finally, in part three, you'll understand how to make the new success model stick in organizational settings. You'll obtain a new model for building inspiring organizations so that you can expand the new success into the organizational systems of business, education, the nonprofit sector, or government institutions.

Along the way, I'll provide exercises and reflections to help you make the new success model stick. At the end of the book, you'll find a resources section with unique personality assessments and resources to integrate the spirit and approaches of this book into your life.

When I was first exposed to the insights and approaches in this book, they deeply resonated with me but they also stretched my mind. I asked myself how to bring these novel ideas into workplace settings. In 2004, I received that insight on a flight from New York to North Carolina, showing me right in front of my eyes the name Conscious Business Institute. I knew then and there that this was what I wanted to dedicate my life to. Since founding the institute in 2005, we've tried and tested the approaches in this book with over 60,000 professionals in organizations with one to 150,000 employees – from fast-moving Silicon Valley startups to the most iconic corporations, including Starbucks, Intel, BMW, and many others.

Were all my clients able to embrace these approaches? No. But for those who did, it profoundly changed their lives. Some were selected for C-level positions in global corporations because their energy and way of being changed, making them better leaders. Others transitioned out of their jobs to create successful businesses of their own, and yet others used the approaches to build human-centric cultures in their organizations.

As you embrace these ideas, I cannot promise where the trajectory of your life will take you. What I will promise is that you'll access a new space of possibility for your life. I wish you an inspiring journey and sincerely hope that this book will allow you to access those places in your life that you've always wanted to explore, but were never quite able to reach.

PART 1
A BETTER WAY TO WORK AND LIVE

CHAPTER 1

The Problem: Upgrading the Way We Work – Succeeding on Our Own Terms

"You cannot solve a problem with the same kind of thinking that created the problem in the first place."
– Albert Einstein

We spend 25 percent of our life at work – more than ninety thousand hours. And yet more than 80 percent of people are disengaged from their work, many of them ready to walk out the front door and never come back if they only knew a better way to earn a living and get ahead. The United Nations declared workplace stress a "global epidemic," costing American businesses more than $300 billion a year. Stanford's organizational development psychologist Jeffrey Pfeffer takes it one step further; in his book *Dying for a Paycheck* he states that our workplaces are literally killing people. And yet, we keep doing business as usual.

The way we work and pursue success isn't working anymore. The story we've been told from an early age – that we'd live a happy and fulfilled life if we just worked hard enough, strived to get ahead, completed a good education, and secured a good position – is not true.

It's not a coincidence that employees started quitting their jobs *en masse*, kicking off the Great Resignation in early 2021. Professionals have long searched for a different, better way to work, for an alternative way to pursue success, which doesn't just fulfill our need to make money and get ahead in life, but also gives us a deeper sense of purpose, fulfillment, and well-being. But how do we get there? We read books about success, take online courses, attend yoga retreats, and – if you're working in a corporation – hire top-notch trainers in an attempt to improve the emotional side of the workplace.

But when we return to the office on Monday morning, not much has changed. Our calendars are still booked with meetings. We're pushing ahead, managing constant deadlines, juggling our personal life with a steadily increasing workload. While yoga retreats and e-courses can nudge us along in our personal lives, they've hardly had any positive impact on the level of stress, dissatisfaction, or lack of meaning that's pervasive in our workplaces around the globe. For the past decades, despite all the perks, beanbags, and free Greek yogurts, the needle on employee happiness and global engagement has barely moved, hovering back and forth between completely unacceptable 12 percent engagement and still lousy 20 percent. The only portion of our work that has seen a steady increase is our level of stress – from 31 percent feeling stressed out on a daily basis in 2009 to over 40 percent in 2020.

There's a deeper issue at play. The widespread yearning for a better way to work and live isn't a personal issue. It's not even a workplace issue. There's a hidden mechanism that's at the root of all our struggle and suffering: our existing model of success. This is the model that most of us have learned to become successful, in our personal lives and in organizations of all sizes. The surprising truth is that our existing model of success is not designed to make us happy. It's actually the reason for our frustration and suffering.

There's a fundamental flaw in the way we conduct business and pursue success that is responsible for *all* the struggle and *all* the suffering in our life. It's responsible for our personal longing for fulfillment and purpose, for the low engagement in our workplaces, and even the conflicts we see when we turn on the daily news.

Excuse Me: You're Barking up the Wrong Tree

For millennia, we've learned to strive for success by following an approach that evolved from our basic survival mechanism: our fear-based fight-or-flight instinct. Consciously or unconsciously, most of us follow a success model designed to prevent pain without consideration of our deeper desires. Our success model doesn't leave room for the expression of our authentic personalities, it doesn't ask what we're passionate about, nor is it designed to help us express our full potential as human beings.

In our culture, the model of success that's deeply ingrained in our thinking follows a simple formula:

$$DO + ACCUMULATE = BECOME$$

DO more and ACCUMULATE more, so
you can BECOME somebody.

From the time we enter school, and often before, we're told to behave or perform in accordance with this success model. We've learned that if we don't comply our chances to make it in the world sharply decline. Our parents or teachers suggest that if we just *do more* and *accumulate* what's important to get ahead, degrees, money, status, property or a family, we'll ultimately *become somebody* or *something* – a doctor, an executive, a wealthy and respected person, or a happy parent.

From an early age, we study subjects that might not spark our interest or take our individual personalities and talents into consideration, only to *accumulate* good grades, and, maybe, *become* an honor student.

By the time we graduate from high school, most of us have already been educated out of our authenticity. With only a distant memory left about who we *really* are, we celebrate a smashing graduation, get the boost of pride and recognition we've been promised, and then continue with the same model undeterred in college: *do* more, work harder, *accumulate* a certificate, title, or degree, so that we *become* an engineer, a massage therapist, or an accountant – not because it inspires us, but because it promises us a "good life."

Once we enter the work world – often until we retire – we work hard and do more, accumulate money, positions, a house, maybe a boat, so that we become a respected personality with a secure lifestyle. It is usually at that time when I receive such emails as this one from Ann, a senior vice president at a global corporation: "Peter, I really need to find out what I want to do with my life." Or from Stefan, a European CEO for a global communications company: "I'm successful, at the top of the food chain, but I can't tell you how often I'm asking myself whether I'm wasting my life."

Author and philosopher Alan Watts says: "All the time, we say to ourselves: The thing is coming. It's coming. It's coming. That great thing. The success you're working for. And then, when you wake up one day and you're about 40 years old, you say to yourself: My God, I've arrived! I'm there. And you don't feel very different from how you've always felt."

Of course, it is possible to become successful with the existing success model. There are many examples of individuals who have accumulated a lot of power and wealth, made it to the top in global corporations, or even become president of a country. But if you look at the life of these individuals holistically, you notice that this model always comes at a cost: breakdowns in their marriage, their relationship to their children, or missing peace of mind.

There's Don, for example, a New York hedge fund manager, who on the outside lives the perfect life with his family in Connecticut. And yet, I get his call, deeply disturbed and under enormous pressure as he wonders how to keep his $40,000 a month lifestyle, the mansion, the school fees, and the social facade so that friends and acquaintances don't turn their back on him.

Or the CEO of a Fortune 100 company who's leading well over 100,000 employees. And yet he feels disconnected from his spouse and sees the centuries-old culture of his organization erode in front of his eyes because he's constantly pushing people to do more, drive revenue higher, and become the number one in the world. How would that daily behavior sit with you if you were his employee, let alone his wife?

Of course, this is not happening to everyone. Maybe you feel that you're living an overall successful and happy life. You've created a good career, and when you come home at night, you have a wonderful family waiting. Even though everything in your life seems good, if you are reading this book, it's likely that there's a deeper awareness that something's missing. Like an itch you can't reach. You know that you could go on living just the way you do, ignore the itch, and focus on refurbishing your kitchen. But deep down, you know the itch won't go away.

As you look closer at those areas where you feel the itch – frustration with work, conflict with family, or missing peace of mind – you'll find that the existing success model is at play. There's something missing that you want to get – to *accumulate* – and you feel you have to *do* something more, something less, or something different to get it.

When you're frustrated with your job, without hesitancy or conscious awareness, your mind refers to our existing success model and immediately suggests that you need to "do" something different to "get there": change your job, take yoga classes, or book a vacation just to get away.

But the existing success model rarely creates the peace or satisfaction we long for. It always urges us to do more or do something different. And since our doing usually originates from the same place of thinking – the mindset that there's something missing and we need to do more to get it – our existing way to pursue success never gets us to the place we yearn for: to truly *be* at peace and expand into the flow of life. As a matter of fact, the stronger we pursue success with the DO – ACCU-MULATE – BECOME approach the farther it takes us away from the life our heart is longing for.

Do We All Use This Success Model?

No, we don't. The existing success model isn't true for everyone. Certainly not for those few who are truly successful doing what they love. While the vast majority of our workforce feels exhausted from treading water, some individuals – five or ten percent in any given organization – are like fish in water, truly enjoying what they do. You can see them around you and if you observe their behaviors, it appears that they're living in the flow – swimming downstream instead of upstream. While ninety or even ninety-five percent keep pushing along, these few individuals seem to defy the existing success model. They don't just like what they do. They live by a different model of success. Whether musician, writer, entrepreneur, or hedge fund manager, these individuals often end up in highly successful positions, not because they work harder or are better at accumulating, but because they're playing another game altogether.

Even though they might not be aware of it, the truly successful individuals follow a different model of success – a success model that's available to every one of us.

We're at a crossroads, both for our personal lives and our businesses: if we choose to continue pursuing success with the DO – ACCUMU-LATE – BECOME model, not much will change. Maybe we'll achieve temporary relief, find ways where we can work from home for a couple of days per week, or, if we're lucky, push ahead with the existing model until we "become" financially independent. Alternatively, we can transition to a different model of success, which allows us to expand into a completely new level of satisfaction, well-being, and flow.

The following chapters provide the pathway to get there. You'll explore a new way to work and live – a way of succeeding that allows you to expand into who you're truly here to be. A Plan B – for yourself, your work, and our world.

CHAPTER 2

The Solution:
A New Model for Success

"I had no idea that being your authentic self could make me as rich as I've become. If I had, I'd have done it a lot earlier."
— Oprah Winfrey

Think about Richard Branson steering his Virgin empire of over 250 companies from his island in the Caribbean, about Oprah Winfrey delivering her TV shows, Nigel Kennedy performing a violin concerto, or Steve Jobs sparking another stroke of genius at Apple. Do you see them "going to work" when they do what they do? Oprah or Kennedy don't watch the clock for the show to be over or for that final chord. If that were the case, whatever they created would feel flat, uninspiring, a means to an end. These individuals can't wait to show up for another day "at work." They're enjoying every moment, present in each inter-action, every note. A vastly different experience compared to today's work world, where so much of what we do is geared toward reaching that final chord. How does Branson's, Oprah's, or Kennedy's experience compare to your workday?

These individuals deliver the proof that there's an alternative way to work where we can access our inherent human potential without constantly pushing on to the next thing or struggling to get ahead. Of course, Kennedy didn't become a virtuoso overnight. Branson didn't start out with 250 companies. There was an enormous amount of work required to get to where these individuals are. But maybe, even early on, delivering a TV interview, inventing a new tech product, or practicing the violin didn't feel like work to them. Maybe they didn't work in the traditional sense to get to where they are now, instead these individuals who seem to enjoy a different, more wholesome level of success followed a different model of success from the get-go – an approach that got them to where they are today. Upon closer examination, they didn't just follow a different approach. They "worked" from a different "place of being" altogether.

If we also worked from this different place of being, it could change everything: from the way we feel about our lives to the way we built organizations and the impact we would make in the world. We'd be able to expand into a level of authentic expression and power that we might not even be aware of right now.

How can we create that level of satisfaction, purpose, and success in our own lives? What's necessary to break away from the existing DO – ACCUMULATE – BECOME success model and still get things done? Before we're able to let go of our existing model of success, we must understand how the new model works. Even more so, we must prime our minds and viscerally experience how the new success model feels so we have the courage to let go of the old model's reins and explore life and success in this different way. We must learn how to install this alternative success model like a new operating system so that we don't fall back into the DO – ACCUMULATE – BECOME model the moment we become frustrated or stressed.

Breaking the Pattern

To break our deeply ingrained patterns of the DO – ACCUMULATE – BECOME success model and create the inner space to shift to an alternative model requires more than better organization or taking a vacation to improve work-life balance. As long as we still think and operate from the existing success model of "doing something different," not much will change. We've all tried it. We might nudge our business or our well-being along, maybe increase sales and feel a bit more at ease, but changing something within the existing model will never allow us to expand into the possibilities the new model of success offers to us.

The new model of success cannot involve "doing" something different. It can't be a model where we're instructed to follow ten steps to create a different outcome. Any behavioral change – being more outgoing, marketing yourself better, becoming a better leader, or never giving up – won't let you transition away from the DO – ACCUMULATE – BECOME success model because it suggests that we *do* more or *do* something different. We reinforce and sink even deeper into the existing model.

To transition to the new model of success requires us to change our thinking – our consciousness. It doesn't require us to *do* anything, but first and foremost to *be*. The new success model represents a new paradigm – a different reality in which we operate. It literally compares to installing a new operating system for the way we live and pursue success. The shift to this new model of success is simple; a welcomed relief. And yet it is as radically profound as the discovery that the earth is round: one thought that changed the trajectory of history, allowing Columbus to consider sailing to the west to reach India instead of sailing eastward, landing in America, and laying the groundwork for all the developments – constructive and destructive – that followed. One different thought – a completely new world.

Shifting our perception to the new success model doesn't make life harder. It doesn't take much work, and we don't have to go anywhere to have it happen. It takes place right between our ears but has the most profound implications for everything we create in our lives – from the way we work and conduct business to the way we govern our countries.

The shift that's required to transition to a new success model follows this formula:

$$BE + DO = HAVE$$

The new success model asks of us to **BE** authentic, to **DO** what our gifts inspire, and, as a consequence, to **HAVE** or **RECEIVE** the *feeling states* we desire to experience in life, such as fulfillment, well-being, abundance, and joy.

As simplistic as it appears, very few people live by this model. For reasons which we'll explore in the following chapters, this model has been evasive or impossible to reach for most people.

But look at Oprah, Richard Branson, or the author Joseph Campbell, and you'll find that in those moments where they're in the flow, they're truly being themselves and expressing their unique gifts and talents. Over and over. Not to attain riches and titles, but because it brings them fulfillment, purpose, and joy. You can sense that Oprah just loves authentic conversations about human growth; Branson is living his passion for adventure and shaking up industries; and Campbell expressed his magic to understand human behavior and to convey it to people in spoken or written words. If you asked any of them what they'd do if they didn't earn any money, they'd probably just stare at you and tell you that they'd continue doing exactly the same thing, because creating meaningful conversations, bringing new ideas into the world, or understanding and writing about human behavior is not what they *do*. It's who they are. Their outside success is not their goal, it's a consequence of how they show up.

Find a person you truly admire, not for the money they've made but for their personality. In those areas where you admire that person, do they focus on "doing more" all the time? Do they go to work, focusing on "accumulating" degrees, titles, or money? Or do they simply and courageously express who they are – their authentic personality, their gifts and talents – and as a consequence achieve success?

I would like you to genuinely feel the difference this new success model makes. If reflecting on the new success model is a purely mental exercise, and your mind tells you, "I got this, let's move on," it'll be a waste of your time – just like discussing how an orange tastes can never compare to the experience of biting into the flesh of a juicy orange. As you read the next paragraphs, I encourage you to keep sensing whether you can detect a shift of energy in your body – whether you feel contraction or expansion or relaxation.

Picture Oprah Winfrey in her show. Imagine how her show would feel if Oprah was hard at work, if she was trying to accomplish something. How would she come across if her primary focus was to get ahead, accumulate money, or receive pats on the back? As you listen to her, how would it feel if she strived to *become* someone or get somewhere, like someone giving a sales pitch to get a business deal? Most likely you're able to feel the tension, pushing, exhaustion, and ultimately the limited success this will yield.

Now, switch scenes. See her being herself on stage; observe how she does what she's really good at, and, as a consequence, she experiences fulfillment, abundance, and a sense of joy in her job. Observe the depth and connection that become possible in that moment – to herself, her interview partner, and the audience – when she shows up authentically. Can you sense how this creates an energy that draws you in, how the entire system – Oprah, her interview partners, and even you – are able to relax? Oprah explains how this affected her financial success: "I had no idea that being your authentic self could make me as rich as I've become. If I had, I'd have done it a lot earlier."

Or look at singer-songwriter Katy Perry. Did she reach her success by focusing her energy on accumulating more? Or does she express her authenticity on stage by doing what her gifts inspire her to do? In her documentary film Perry says: "I've always been ambitious since I was nine years old and that was never going to change. That's exactly me . . . . Everyone wanted to change me along the way and I've stuck to my guns. My first record company tried to mold me into the next Avril Lavigne, then the next Kelly Clarkson, when all I wanted was to be the first Katy Perry."

Let me be clear: I'm not suggesting that Oprah, Perry, or the others in our world who live by the new success model don't face struggle or conflict in their lives. We all do. It's part of our human existence. What I'd like you to consider is that where these individuals experience the sense of flow, abundance, or full expression of their personalities we're all seeking, they're following the BE – DO – HAVE success model. And in those areas where they don't, they also fall back into the DO – ACCUMULATE – BECOME model of success.

You can see this play out in exactly the same way in your life. Search for an area in your life where you feel completely at ease, without any worry, fear, or frustration. When you take a walk in the park, look into your child's eyes, or pet your cat. In those areas where you're in the flow of life, you are actually being yourself, doing what you want to do right now, experiencing joy, connection, freedom, or ease. You're not doing or accumulating anything, not trying to get anywhere. We *know* how the new success model feels. That's why we recognize the pull when we put our head on the pillow at night. Part of us knows and wants to get back to that feeling. Yet, in a blink of an eye without conscious awareness, we flip right back into the DO – ACCUMULATE – BECOME model. Our mind takes over and sorts through everything we need to accomplish the next day: the presentation for your boss, the marketing campaign, the house payments, or the many other things on our never-ending to-do list.

Be the Change – Don't Do the Change

When we set out to change something in our life or when we're confronted with a problem or conflict we usually ask: "What can I *do* differently?" When your boss gives you a negative appraisal, your first response is: "What do I need to do differently or better?" In a conflict with your spouse, it's not much different. More often than not, you want the other to *do* something differently. *If you just stopped leaving your clothes lying around,* you think, *I'd be okay.* We constantly think and operate within the framework of the DO – ACCUMULATE – BECOME success model: *do* something different, *get* the relationship or praise we want, *become* promoted or appreciated.

But look around. It's not working. Even if our spouse puts away their clothes, it's usually just a few days before we want them to *do* something else differently. Maybe this time to clean up the dishes. We repeat this cycle because even if our spouse does something different on the outside, it cannot give us the appreciation or understanding that we have been seeking all along. Even if you work extra hard for your boss, reach the promotion you want, you still find yourself at your new desk, concerned about the next appraisal or what might happen if you stopped pushing yourself and eased up a bit.

Doing something different without *Being* the required change is like rearranging deck chairs on the Titanic. If we're lucky, it manipulates the immediate situation, but it doesn't provide the lasting transformation we're seeking in our personal lives, such as reducing overwork, stress, or dissatisfaction. And it also can't provide the transformation we need in our world – to create businesses that operate more purpose-driven and sustainably or to reduce the level of conflict between countries.

If we continue trying to change things only by *Doing* something different, we won't create a lasting impact because all of our *doing* originates from our *being* – from the way we see the world and ourselves. Look at the new success model again. If we want to HAVE something different in our life, say, a fulfilling relationship, everything we DO in that relationship – the way we communicate, support, or react – originates in who we are BEING.

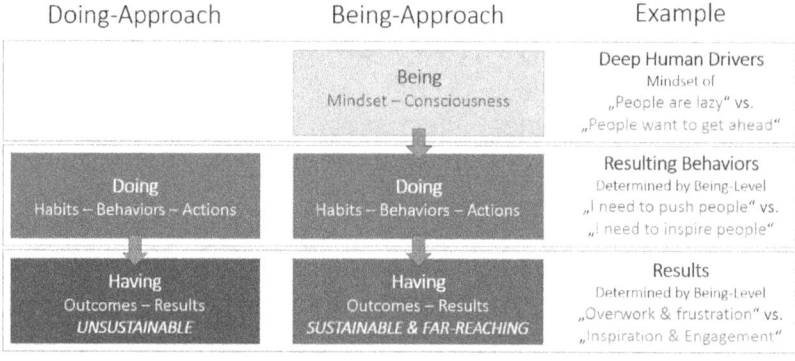

Graphic 1: The impact of our level of being

If you think that your boss is inadequate or incapable and needs to change, everything you say to him will be filtered through that perception. Everything you communicate, even your body language, will reflect your inner reality. Consequently, the results (what you will HAVE) in your relationship with your boss will be negative as well. If, however, you manage to shift your perception and you enter the conversation with a more positive mindset about him, a mindset of possibility, appreciation, or understanding, even if you just appreciate his haircut or the suit he's wearing, everything you say will filter through that particular lens. Consequently, how you relate to your boss is much more likely to be positive.

To shift to the new BE – DO – HAVE success model doesn't require us to *do* something different. It requires us to change who we are *being* in this world. As a result, we can finally create the experiences we are yearning for.

But What About Money?

At this point, people commonly ask about money. "This all sounds great, and it would be wonderful if I could *be* myself all the time," they say, "but if I want to make a living and put bread on the table, I do need to eventually roll up my sleeves and *do*." There's no debating: if we want to achieve or create anything in life, it ultimately requires some *doing*. The new success model does not state that we don't get things done. It suggests that we do things from a place of enjoyment and love. Not because we have to, but because we want to. I'll address in more detail how we can create that "inspired doing" in chapters 9 and 11.

Still, if you want to embrace the new success model, your mindset around money will be one of the biggest obstacles to address. To a large extent, money has become the representation for safety, power, and freedom in our world. If that would be taken away from you and you'd have to scrape by in challenging circumstances, there's no question that life would start to suck. Our relationship with money reaches deep into our human psyche, so we'll address this topic in detail at a later stage. For now, let's just take an initial glance.

When I work with professionals in the United States, unless they're high up in the value chain, virtually everyone brings up money when speaking about happiness and success. Financial freedom is at the top of the wish list for many, driven by the notion that if we become financially free, we can finally BE who we want to be, DO what we love to do, and HAVE the joy, freedom, and peace of mind we're looking for. Essentially, if we become financially free, we tell ourselves, we can finally switch to the BE – DO – HAVE success model. Unfortunately, that doesn't happen for many. And statistics show that the wealthy – after an initial spike of happiness – don't end up much happier than the average middle-class American.

In western European countries, the yearning is often a different one: how to find a job where I can be myself, do what I love, *and* earn money along the way. I'm not sure if it's a different work ethic or whether Europeans miss out on the American narrative of financial success. Either way, money is still the obstacle – possibly one of the biggest dilemmas that's holding us back from creating the life we want.

Even if we've accomplished everything – a good job with steady income, a comfortable lifestyle – how can we move to the BE – DO – HAVE success model without giving that up? Essentially, we want to stay on the carousel while adding a deeper sense of Being to our life. But as we're going around and around on the carousel, so many times we're unaware that what got us there is that we had it all backward in the first place. We hoped that once we *had* all these things – the good job, the house, the prep schools for our kids – that it would eventually allow us to *do* what we love and ultimately *be* happy.

Here's the conundrum we're up against: if we truly want to create success in our lives, can we trust that if we're authentic, if we express our unique talents, if we're fully ourselves, money will follow?

For decades of our life, we've repeatedly learned and witnessed that if we work hard, get a degree from a good school, join a good firm, we'll at least get some of the love, acknowledgment, and appreciation that we've been promised. We *know* that the old success model is a proven way to get us there. But we haven't been told the fine print: the cost of the DO – ACCUMULATE – BECOME model. What we do not know yet is whether the new success model actually works. Our mind, our body, our emotional system doesn't know the outcome. We haven't seen in our families, workplaces, or the media that the new success model actually works.

Just take a stroll down Madison Avenue and you'll see that if you just bought that new Prada bag, you'll be acknowledged by others. There's no billboard nudging you to expand into yourself and enjoy the fresh air. As individuals blazing the trail for a new era, this is an uncertainty we must confront. It's exactly in those moments of uncertainty when we don't know how our future looks that we can create a new life order. On our way to the new success model, it will be normal that one part of us knows that we can live abundantly with the BE – DO – HAVE model while another part warns us that we might run out of money and lose everything we've built so far.

Ask yourself: if you knew exactly what you would get if you switched to the BE – DO – HAVE success model – happiness, satisfaction, and a sense of abundance – in exactly the same way you know that you'll get appreciation, acknowledgment, and support when you follow the existing model, would you hesitate to make the switch? Wouldn't you have made the switch a long time ago? But we don't know. We haven't been told in school to "be abundantly yourself and abundance will follow," or to focus our energy on developing what we love to do. Most of us haven't even learned what authenticity really means, what our deeper purpose is, or who we're here to *be*. So, we revert to what's familiar: *do* more, keep *accumulating*, hoping that we'll eventually "get there."

But now, with our world at a crossroads, it's time to reconsider. What if your authenticity is actually the foundation for true success? What would be possible if you knew how to express your authenticity in the world, and that peace, abundance, and well-being would follow if you did exactly that? Would you wait another day?

Reflection: Try the New Success Model on For Size

Take a deep breath.

Pick a situation in which you feel frustration or stress. Your workload, your coworker's behavior, or something where you are not enjoying the process.

Ask yourself: as you attempt to change that situation, what are you looking to get – to accumulate? Is it recognition, money, happiness, maybe understanding?

Next, what will you become once you have that? Once your workload eases, your boss changes their behavior, or you create something with ease and joy, what will you become? At peace, happy, or successful?

Now, look at the strategy you've come up with to change the situation. Most likely, you've come up with needing to do something to create what you want.

Now let's shift. Bring the situation back to mind. What would happen if there's nothing you needed to *do*? If you simply showed up fully present in that situation – if you literally expanded into being yourself without the need to alter the situation? Just for now.

Your workload is still there, your boss still behaves the way she does. But now, you're okay just being yourself in that situation. Can you feel your body relax?

Ask yourself what you'd do if you just brought your authentic personality and your unique gifts into the situation – not because you want something but because it would bring you satisfaction, connection, or maybe happiness.

As people do this, they often describe that they're accessing a new place of centeredness and power, which was not available to them before. I hope you had a similar experience. Be mindful that this is not an overnight solution. The shift to a more expanded state of *being* isn't like flipping a switch. It takes practice. It's an unfamiliar state for many of us, and like most of us, you'll likely slip back. It's okay.

The Plan BE Online Course

Explore the Plan BE Online Course to go deeper and to apply the ideas and insights in this book to your work and life. In the course, you'll find thirty bite-sized videos to help deepen your understanding of the Plan BE material, as well as insightful exercises and reflections to make it stick in your life, including the unique Conscious Business Institute Personality Color Assessments to uncover a more wholesome understanding of who you're here to be.

To learn more about the Plan BE Online Course, visit *learn.plan-be.us* or scan below QR code. As an owner of this book, use the coupon code "MYPLANBE" to get the reduced rate.

CHAPTER 3

How We Decide: What's Holding Us Back

"The human emotional system can be roughly broken down into two elements. Fear and love. Love is of the soul. Fear is of the personality."

– Gary Zukav

In 2010, Michael, a vice president at one of the leading global automotive companies was tasked by his board to come up with a solution for a challenging problem. The company was developing new, three-cylinder engines to make their cars more fuel efficient. When the production team examined the prototypes, they realized that the new engines didn't just sound like a sewing machine, they also caused noise and vibration inside the vehicle that made it uncomfortable for passengers to drive the car. Michael and his team of over one hundred audio and sound engineers had to find a solution and present it to the board of the corporation.

A strong, even-keeled man and seasoned leader, Michael had a reputation among colleagues to be driven, but also kind and people-centric. He cared for his team members and stated many times in presentations that culture and people are the most important asset of an organization. His convictions were supported by his positive relationship to his wife and stepson, and, during his career, he had noticed how his human-centric view of the world helped deepen connections and build a collaborative spirit across his teams.

When the board asked him to deliver a solution for the sound issue, everything shifted. Like flipping a switch, Michael became determined to deliver a perfect solution for the board. As a matter of fact, he wanted his presentation to be so impactful that the board would give him applause for his work, something that isn't common in any board room, let alone in a traditional, engineering-focused automotive company.

For weeks, he laser-focused his team's attention on finding the solution and creating the perfect demonstration. He was so "in it" that he didn't notice how his behavior had shifted: he was stretched to the limit, he pressured his team to deliver the results he wanted, and his people-first values were overridden by his personal goal to succeed.

When it was time to deliver, Michael was pumped up to give the perfect presentation. He achieved his goal: the board gave him a standing ovation.

When I met with him a few days later in his office, I could still feel his adrenaline pulsing through his body. But alongside his success he felt sadness. By the time we met, he realized that he had completely overridden one of his main principles: to put people first. His relentless push for perfection had alienated many on his team, eroding trust and collaboration. But it saddened him most that his perfectionism had caused a distancing from his stepson, who had withdrawn from Michael throughout the weeks and now said that he hadn't enjoyed being around his stepfather. After Michael shared his story with me, he sat in silence for a while, digesting the past weeks. Then he asked me, "Why do we fall back into the old success model, keep pushing along and even throw those things out of the window that are important to us, *even* if we know exactly that it's not the 'right' thing to do?"

We all know this scenario: Like an invisible rubber band pulling us, we overwork, even though we know it harms our well-being; we dig our heels into the ground in conversations to be right, even though we know it harms the relationship; we strive to get the job we want, even though we know it doesn't bring us the happiness we're looking for. We're seeking a sense of completeness, connection, and well-being, and yet we keep doing more, pushing ahead, trying to get somewhere.

There's a hidden mechanism that prevents us from shifting to the new success model and creating a life that fulfills our deeper aspirations. What's holding us back is a deeply ingrained model of behavior that we are not aware of, and yet it governs many of our decisions in businesses, governments, and even in our personal relationships.

I call this mechanism the Model of Dominance & Subservience. This behavioral model lies at the root of all our stress and struggle; it is the hidden force that continuously pulls us back into following the existing model of success. This model suggests a rather simplistic and primitive approach to cope with or circumvent the fundamental problems, fears, and frustrations that we all face as human beings – from threats to our physical well-being to the fear of running out of money or being rejected by someone we love.

When we pursue success with the DO – ACCUMULATE – BECOME approach, the Model of Dominance & Subservience is the driving force behind our actions. To this day, this model governs many aspects of society, from global institutions to personal relationships. Whenever our behaviors are influenced by this model, we operate from a scarcity mindset fueled by the principal belief that there's not enough of what we need – not enough food, not enough love, not enough money, not enough time. And as a result, we spend much of our time and energy accumulating these limited resources to maintain our well-being. Throughout the course of our lives, we've been raised and educated with this model. Passed down from generation to generation, the belief that there's not enough has become our lens of perception, distorting our view of ourselves and the world around us, ultimately suggesting to us that *we are not enough*. Even though we might not be aware of it, this scarcity mindset is familiar to all of us. It turns up in your life when your boss tells you that your work isn't good enough, when your spouse complains that you don't spend enough time with them, or when you think that you don't work hard enough.

Of course, we don't use the Model of Dominance & Subservience at all times. Certainly not when we're "in the flow of life" (which we'll explore later) or when we operate from the new success model. But when scarcity dominates our thinking – when we operate from the mindset that there's not enough of something we deem important for us or our survival – we unconsciously flip a switch in our brain and the Model of Dominance & Subservience dominates our choices.

Our Three Fundamental Fears

This model of behavior is driven by three fundamental fears that have been humanity's steadfast companions for millennia:

> The loss of love, affection, and support – our fear that we'll be rejected by the tribe.

> The loss of safety we might require when we're in need – our fear that our life might be in danger.

The loss of power in case we need to fend off enemies or domination by others – our fear that we're not powerful enough to meet our physical needs.

In today's world, these fears usually don't show up in the same way as they did in tribal times. Instead of the raw fear from a saber-toothed tiger attack, we "only" feel frustration about our workload or worry about making our monthly mortgage payment. We work away on a presentation for some colleagues on a normal Wednesday, cruising along as we create a pretty slide deck. The next day, dressed up and ready to go, we stand in front of our audience of fifty colleagues, ready to share our ideas. Suddenly, our hands get sweaty, our heart beats faster, and our voice loses firmness. One of our fundamental fears comes alive and alarms us: What will others think? Will they stop appreciating or supporting us? Will we get rejected? Will we be good enough?

Whenever the Model of Dominance & Subservience controls our thinking, we feel driven to avoid one or more of the three potential losses: power, safety, or love. Many times we're not even aware of what's driving our choices or exactly when this model takes over our behaviors. Yet for most of us not a day goes by that we don't think or act in a way that's governed by this model: someone in the street doesn't return your smile, withholding the affection you were hoping to receive; your boss criticizes your work in a feedback meeting, raising the concerns whether your job is in danger; you spend the weekend working because you think that if your results aren't good enough, you won't get the support from your boss for the promotion; or your spouse engages in a wide-eyed conversation with another man or woman, leaving you wondering whether your relationship is as solid as it used to be. In those moments, whether we're aware of it or not, our mind fires up its fight-or-flight circuitry, sending a signal that something important to us is at risk – that we might lose our job, our salary, our spouse, or appreciation and love from others.

Once we operate from a scarcity mindset, we're left with two options. We can give in and dwell in our perceived reality that there's not enough money, we're not good enough, or we're not safe. We become subservient. Or we can roll up our sleeves and change the situation in an attempt to dominate our environment.

When someone cuts you off in traffic and you get furious, your emotional response indicates that the Model of Dominance & Subservience has kicked into gear. You either swallow your anger and remain quiet, or you lay on the horn, get out of your car, and start handing it back to the sucker – even if you just do so in your mind. Dominant or subservient. Either way, in this very moment you're *doing* something to *become* something – you swallow your anger to become peaceful, superior, or "the good person," or you lash out at the person to become powerful or "right." You're not simply *being* anymore, present and aware of what's going on inside of you. You're manipulating outside circumstances to match your perceived inner needs – to be powerful, safe, and loved.

Similarly, when your boss criticizes your team's performance in a meeting and you feel your blood pressure rising, you can either remain quiet or you can defend your actions, providing an excuse for why the performance was below par or explaining that your boss didn't set clear expectations. As long as we hold unresolved emotions while remaining quiet, we become subservient. In providing explanations or defending ourselves, we attempt to move into a dominant position. As long as we're governed by the Model of Dominance & Subservience, we eliminate the possibility of a win-win scenario. In our mind, we must either dominate the situation or be dominated. It's me against you. We either win or we lose.

When the Model of Dominance & Subservience governs our behaviors, we cannot simply accept the situation that's in front of us. We feel compelled, often beyond our control, to at least try to manipulate the situation to avoid the three fundamental fears – the loss of love, safety, or power – even if it means hurting a loved one. Taking basic physics into account, whenever we manipulate something, there's resistance, resistance causes friction, and friction creates stress. Whenever the Model of Dominance & Subservience is present, we eliminate the possibility of balance and flow.

As long as the Model of Dominance & Subservience governs much of our lives and our workplaces, we're not living in our true power as human beings or expressing our full abilities. We're not taking responsibility for our behaviors or even understanding the deeper motivators and reasons for our behaviors. If we pursue success with the existing model, our mind is so caught up in meeting its perceived needs that it's not paying much attention to the impact of our behaviors on our bodies, our psyches, or the world. As a result, our bodies are exhausted, our minds are in a chronic state of overwhelm, and our environment is suffering.

Since our existing model of success is shaped by the belief that "there's not enough," whether we're aware of it or not, we spend much of our time and energy working harder to accumulate or secure the resources that we believe are essential for our survival. In earlier days these resources were food, shelter, and safety; today it is primarily money. In the Model of Dominance & Subservience, the few people who control the limited resources that are essential for our survival obtain a disproportionate amount of power. In our current success model, the more money you have, the more power you have.

How Dominance & Subservience Impacts Your Life

Look at any challenging situation in your life, an argument with a family member or an issue with a coworker. At some level you'll find someone dominating and another person or group of people being subservient to that dominator. This pattern is visible everywhere in our world. We see it in nations fighting over oil or water, seeking to dominate scarce natural resources. We see it in terrorists blowing themselves up to instill fear in others and gain power for their cause, even through sacrificing their own lives. We see it when we pressure employees to meet quarterly sales projections. Maybe you use the principles of dominance to assert your sense of power by resisting your boss's demands. You may see it in arguments with your spouse, when both of you try to prove that your position is *right*. Even our children have quickly learned how to use dominance by throwing a temper tantrum to get the newest video game some other child got from his parents.

In those areas of our lives where the Model of Dominance & Subservience governs our choices, there will always be scarcity and struggle. Upon closer examination, we'll find that it is *the* underlying cause of most suffering in our lives, it leads to the highest levels of conflict and lack of engagement in organizations, and it is the reason for destructive and fear-based decisions that shape the world around us.

When we're overworked or involved in an argument, we usually don't see our emotional reaction – our exhaustion, outrage, judgment, frustration, or withdrawal – for what it is: the deep-rooted human fear that we might lose love, support, or power. Instead, some people's strategy is to go numb, keep working, or medicate by eating or watching TV. Others blow a fuse and embark on an emotional wave that turns their behaviors and choices into a roller-coaster ride for themselves and people around them. We've all seen it when people change right in front of our eyes as if someone flipped a switch: some of us become angry and aggressive, some manipulative and blaming, and others become quiet and withdrawn. As we attempt to solve the problem through dominating the situation or becoming subservient, our decisions and actions don't originate from a neutral, empowered position anymore but from a distorted perception that our very existence is threatened. Our decisions are "out of power," and the majority of our energy is allocated to getting out of this survival situation – oftentimes at the cost of others' health or our own.

This instinctive fight-or-flight reaction is not our fault. It is part of human nature – a survival mechanism honed over the course of millennia to cope with life-threatening situations: when a bear attacks us, when someone points a weapon at us, or when a fire threatens to harm our family. While this fast and powerful instinctual reaction is helpful in life-threatening situations and protects the well-being and survival of our species, its high intensity is not suited for solving day-to-day conflicts and challenges like worrying about money or getting caught in an argument with our boss. What if every time the fuel lamp lit up in your car, instead of using it as a subtle reminder to keep your eyes out for a gas station, you would break out in utter panic, creating a crisis situation for the entire family riding with you. When we choose the roles of dominator or subservient, our behaviors go on autopilot. We're literally "out of our mind." Everything we think, say, or do originates from a scarcity-based, fight-or-flight mindset that ultimately causes a crisis for our environment, other people, or our own well-being.

Many of us have spent so much time and effort maneuvering our role in this fragile system that we don't know who we really are anymore, let alone what we feel inside of us. I can't count the number of people that have confessed to me that they're so busy focusing on the outcome, functioning in their jobs, or reacting to the world around them, that they've forgotten what makes them happy or can't remember the last time they laughed so hard they couldn't stop. Our current success model doesn't leave much time to relax. It keeps us busy maneuvering the whitewater of life's constant ups and downs. As a result, we don't have the time or may not even know how to look into ourselves – what's really going on inside of us, why we feel this evasive sense of emptiness, and what we can do about it. And without knowing what's going on inside of us, the intimacy (into-me-see), the sense of belonging, connection, and understanding we all search for remains beyond our reach.

Why We Keep Following This Model

If this success model is so destructive, why do we still follow its drum beat? Quite simply, because we don't see an alternative. The Model of Dominance & Subservience is so deeply ingrained in the fabric of our culture that, from our early childhood onwards, it just feels like the normal and "natural" way to behave. It's the language of success we learn. Growing up with this model all around us we even unintentionally use it as parents to raise our children, for example, when we tell them they're too loud or do something wrong. In our schools we use it to educate our youth when we tell them that they have to make certain grades to get ahead. And in the business world we apply it to keep our employees in line or have them meet management's sales targets. Most of us never even imagine there could be an alternative approach to success.

Even though the Model of Dominance & Subservience may sound very black-and-white, my intention is not to judge the dominators, nor do I want to victimize the subservient. My intention is far from compartmentalizing either role because they are both inherent in our human nature, just as they are in the animal world. We usually don't have bad intentions when making money, amassing material belongings, or striving for a role of power and influence during our career. As a matter of fact, in all of the people and organizations I've worked with, I have yet to find a manager who was driven by bad intentions.

When I was scouting for and investing in the best semiconductor companies as a venture capitalist, I certainly hoped that they'd become leaders, maybe even dominators, of a specific market. I didn't invest with bad intentions nor with an awareness about the negative impact these companies might have on the environment or the leadership's negative impact on its employees. Like all of us, I was just doing what I needed to do to get the job done. When I asked business school graduates why they wanted to join investment firms on Wall Street, they simply stated that they wanted to make some money. Nothing wrong with that. In most cases, our motivation is not to dominate – at least not consciously – but to simply get ahead in life or to provide for our family. We compare ourselves to our neighbors, their houses, and how far they have made it in their lives, and all we want is not to fall behind.

We do what feels "natural" to us. We simply speak the "language of success" that we're trained in without examining our deeper motivators or fears that drive our decisions. Most of the time, we create our roles as dominator or subservient innocently, without fully understanding the impact on others, how this model reduces the productivity in organizations, how it actually reduces the safety we are seeking, or how it even creates our ulcers. Conversely, we can't even fathom how the quality of our lives would improve if we stopped following this model.

Our Formula for Success: An 8,000-Year-Old Model

To understand the far-reaching tentacles of this model, let's take a journey back to when we solidified this inner wiring for Dominance & Subservience. The roots of our success model go back to the Neolithic Revolution, about 8,000 years ago, to the time when we formed an agrarian society. Imagine life before that time, when we lived as hunter-gatherers with little or no need to accumulate possessions or surplus of food. Because we had to remain nomadic as hunter-gatherers and follow the food as needed, material possessions or status symbols – permanent housing, elaborate weapons, or the extra Prada purse – were obstacles. In fact, as tribal people we had no concept of accumulating food or material goods at all because hoarding a shed full of food or extra clothes impeded the tribe's mobility and made us vulnerable. In terms of leadership, tribal leaders didn't exert authority over other members of the tribe, and no single individual had an economic advantage. It was an egalitarian society. There was no reason to compare the size of your tent to your brother's. The tribal structure was too lean to support full-time leaders or bureaucrats. Land ownership wasn't invented yet, and the entire tribe, working collectively and cooperatively, defended the safety and well-being of all its members.

There was a mind-altering, unimaginable difference compared with today's world: as hunter-gatherers we mastered our individual survival skills and contributed them for the benefit of the entire tribe. Although we were aware of the dangers around us, we held a mindset of abundance. When anthropologists researched the remaining nomadic cultures in Africa and Australia, tribal members laughed at them when they asked why they didn't manage their food better: "Why would we, if we can get more tomorrow!" Unlike today, as hunter-gatherers we knew deep down that Mother Earth would provide us with everything we needed for our survival, regardless of our race, gender, IQ, or whether we were a complete dropout that enjoyed getting high on fermented fruits. We instinctively knew that there was enough and consequently that *we were enough*. We held a deep sense that we'll be okay – an inner feeling that many of us have lost in today's world and hope to rekindle by accumulating financial wealth.

Life radically changed with the development of the agrarian society. We settled in one place and started *owning* land and other material goods. For the first time, people accumulated the resources that were necessary for survival, namely food and water. A few individuals started monopolizing food and other resources; this new "elite" shifted into a dominating role: landowners who controlled large areas of land obtained authority over others, while at the same time providing others with work and ensuring people's safety. Over the course of centuries, our focus of life shifted from contributing our gifts and talents to the tribe's well-being as hunter-gatherers to focusing more and more time and energy on dominating the resources – food, land, and other material possessions we needed to survive in the agrarian society.

From that point in history, work-life balance became an issue. As hunter-gatherers, we surprisingly had more leisure time and greater amounts of daytime sleep than in any other stage of society. If you did everything right – if you didn't get eaten by a hungry bear on your way back from hunting – you only devoted an average of two to four hours per day to fulfill all your basic needs. The remaining time you were able to rest in camp, visit other camps, entertain visitors, or – especially if you were a man – dance! A relaxed lifestyle compared with today, where we work eight or more hours, commute another hour on top of shopping for and preparing our food.

Where Mother Earth previously provided for our needs, as agrarians we became more dependent on a dominating individual. Before, we lived our lives with an awareness of affluence and abundance as hunter-gatherers, but the newly man-made and institutionalized scarcity – that we might not be able to make a living because we're not "good enough to serve the landlord" or don't have enough food – now intensified our human need for safety, appreciation, and support. While natural disasters or attacks from a saber-toothed tiger were our primary safety concerns as hunter-gatherers, in the Middle Ages we were lucky not to get slaughtered by a tin-armored stranger before dusk.

More and more, our survival depended on other people and material possessions: we needed someone with access to food, people who could provide us with work, shelter, and protection. This continues right up to the present time where many depend on a regular paycheck from a "dominator" to survive in the world. The increasing dependency on a dominator had a sobering psychological impact on us: we started valuing ourselves according to how the dominator valued us, believing that this was the best way to ensure our safety and access to the resources we needed for survival. For many centuries, our labor was paid with commodities – with bartering for grains or animal products – but over time the movers and shakers realized that it would be much easier to trade and accumulate wealth with portable valuables. Initially, those included beads, shells, salt, peppercorns, or precious metals, which ultimately became today's money.

Even now, if what we do for work today (say a strawberry picker) is not highly valued by the dominator, then we can't sell our skills and we barely make enough money to pay for food and shelter. If we have a skill that is more valued by a dominator (being a doctor, for example) we usually have enough money to survive and thrive. And at the far end of the scale, if we manage to accumulate a great deal of money, we have the freedom and power to buy whatever we want, and even control the "value" of others around us. To a large extent, money has become the symbol of value – reflecting our value as individuals – which is usually completely divorced from our value as a person. Every day, politicians, movies, magazines, billboards, or ten-step success programs suggest to us that we'll be happier, more lovable, and more valuable the more money we make, the bigger house we have, or the fancier car we drive.

Go through the corridors of your workplace. When was the last time people were truly recognized and valued for who they are – without judgments, expectations, or consideration of their position or job? We've internalized this value system so deeply that our material wealth has become a reflection of how valuable we perceive ourselves to be and vice versa. If you don't believe in your own value, it is likely that your material world – your job, your relationships, or your finances – directly reflect that belief back to you, no matter how hard you work. Try walking up to your boss and asking for a doubling of your salary. Most likely, your entire nervous system will cringe and deem it unrealistic. But who determines your value?

Since in the western world much of our identity, self-confidence, and personal value is largely tied to money – even if many of us aren't consciously aware of it – the Model of Dominance & Subservience justifies everything for the purpose of getting wealthy, or at least making sure that we keep making enough money. Even if we have strong values and convictions, we might hold onto a job far longer than we want to because it ensures a regular paycheck. Tom, a senior leader at a global corporation, built his 750-person team based on the conviction that his employees are capable, engaged, purpose-driven, and willing to give their best. He was even aware of the Model of Dominance & Subservience and its pitfalls. And yet, once his line managers pressured him to meet higher sales targets, his values went out the door. He overworked himself and started pushing and controlling his employees. And on a global level, we've known for decades that the way we live, consume, and pollute is not sustainable for our planet. In 2022, Earth Overshoot Day – the day when our use of earth's natural resources exceeds what the planet can regenerate during that year – was July 28. We're using nearly twice the renewable resources that are available to us, every year. Yet, there's no meaningful change in sight as long as the existing model of thinking pushes individuals, businesses, or governments to accumulate more money and power.

We know that things need to change. And yet, when we're stressed or worried, we click back into our default tracks and start rolling along – just like a train in set tracks. It may even appear that the Model of Dominance & Subservience has weakened. Aren't we living fairly good and content lives? Most of us never have to go to war or worry that our home will be looted by a neighboring army. In the western world, (especially if you're a white male) some of the obvious suppression by the dominators has been eliminated. But despite all the progress, this model of success still governs large parts of our culture. It's not a model that softens. Since it's determined by the wiring in our brain, we either operate according to it, or we don't.

With this model governing large portions of our behaviors and choices, we might become rich or climb the corporate ladder. We might even become president of a nation. Plenty of examples. But we'll never be able to expand into our full authenticity, nor will we be able to create organizations, countries, or even personal relationships that allow everyone to flourish. If we continue to pursue success with the DO – ACCUMULATE – BECOME model, not much will change.

Ultimately, each one of us – and humanity as a whole – is left with two options.

One, to face the increasing challenges ahead of us with the existing success model – to push even harder, cut costs, develop new laws and tighter regulations, continue manipulating the increasing changes and complexities of our world, and assert more pressure on others to change. Or option two, to transition to the new model of success, which opens to a completely new level of satisfaction, performance, and happiness

– another room of possibility we somehow know exists but have never been able to access.

Many of us are looking for an alternative way to work and live. We take yoga retreats and mindfulness courses, we develop new strategies, even attempt to change company cultures to create more inspiring and purpose-driven work environments. But as long as we return to the existing system of work on Monday morning, with our consciousness dominated by the existing model of success, we cannot expect lasting change. We'll continue to face the same conflicts, the same frustration, struggle, and political maneuvering. What's missing is a clear path to the new model of success, a step-by-step guide that would allow us to break the existing code and make the new operating system stick.

CHAPTER 4

Breaking the Code: Your Authenticity and the New Model for Success

"Out beyond ideas of wrongdoing and rightdoing, there is a field. I'll meet you there. When the soul lies down in that grass, the world is too full to talk about."
— *Rumi*

In a world largely driven by the existing success model, it can be daunting to drift from the mainstream and transition to a new model of being and succeeding. It's an even bigger challenge to withstand the ever-present pull of the deeply ingrained Model of Dominance & Subservience. During this and the following chapters, I'll break down the new BE – DO – HAVE model for your life, starting with the first part: to Be Authentic.

Why is your state of *Being* so important if you want to expand your sense of fulfillment, satisfaction, and abundance? And what does authenticity have to do with reaching that expanded state? Let's examine what your authenticity really is and how you can discover it.

On an early autumn morning in 1997, I found myself in a small, cottage-style house in Carmel, California, sitting across from someone that – within a few hours – would profoundly change the course of my life.

Shortly before, I had sold the shares in my software company, and then my first wife, Jeanine, and I had retreated to Carmel to reflect about the next steps in our lives. We only intended to stay for a few weeks. But as I made Carmel the base for my new business, weeks turned into months, and months turned into years.

Aside from building our "regular life," Jeanine and I were driven by a deeper question: how do we create outstanding success in the outer world, combined with a deep sense of fulfillment and joy in our inner world? We were wondering whether purpose played an important role in reaching true success. And if it did, what was our purpose? To find out, we embarked on a fascinating research tour, traveling weeks at a time to meet with extraordinary individuals from around the world – from the US to South America to Europe – who lived and succeeded off the beaten paths of society.

What interested me in those meetings was whether these individuals followed the same paradigm for creating success in their lives that most of us do or if they had an ingredient to success that most of us weren't aware of. We sought out over ninety individuals that seemed to defy the existing success model: well-known artists, top technology entrepreneurs, medical intuitives, well-known authors, psychics, and shamans from Native American, African, Hawaiian, and South American traditions. What was their secret to living in what seemed to be a beautiful flow and alignment with the world around them?

Toward the end of our meetings, we usually asked these individuals for others they would recommend we include in our research.

When several of them told us that we *had* to include Rob, who only lived a few blocks from us, we asked him for a meeting. The times he suggested didn't work for me, so Jeanine went by herself. When she returned home, she was transformed. For months she had struggled with chronic pain, which dampened her energy and ability to move. But now she flung the door open, excitedly jumping up and down with boundless energy. With lit up eyes and a beaming smile she told me, "Peter, you have to schedule a session with this man. It was incredible." Seeing her full of energy and seemingly without any pain after a two-hour conversation with a stranger, I picked up the phone and scheduled the appointment.

When I arrived at Rob's Carmel cottage, he offered me a seat in a big, comfortable leather chair. I could still smell the salty marine layer hovering above Carmel that morning, calming and muffling the sounds around us. When Rob sunk into his leather chair across from me, he looked like an oversized, six-foot-four teddy bear with a burly beard, thick curly hair tamed into a ponytail, and dressed in a bright red and green Hawaiian shirt. He smiled at me with kind eyes, asking me whether I wanted some water. "You like moving your body, so feel free to take off your shoes and fidget, if you need." Wondering how he knew that about me, I followed his suggestion, not knowing what else I could expect. To make myself comfortable, I glanced around the room – the beautiful oil paintings of a single white Calla Lily and a sleeping beauty; small, cottage-style windows facing a wild, lush garden; a high-beam ceiling. I thought, *This big man in this little house is like Gandalf living with the Hobbits.*

And then, with not much further small talk, Rob jumped right in. Without having ever heard or seen anything of me, he told me who I was here to *be* during this lifetime. "You are a Yellow, Violet with Tan," he said.

A what? With what?

"Violets are the visionaries and purpose-driven leaders in our world," he continued. "Violets are here to make a difference. These are the Gandhis, Martin Luther King Jr.s, Nelson Mandelas, or J.F. Kennedys of our world. You see what's not working in our world and what needs to change. Your job is to lead the way in providing people with a different approach to the way we work. The jobs you've had so far have been very frustrating for you, because you know they aren't nourishing for the soul, and you also know that there's a better way to work and conduct business."

His words struck me as though someone had hit a Japanese gong next to my ear. How was he able to see what I had felt for so many years? First at Accenture and then in my own company, I had observed how dysfunctional the way we do business is. My deepest desire was to find a way to succeed that would feed my soul; I just didn't know whether that was possible. I deeply resonated with his description, but what did he mean by telling me I was a yellow, violet with tan?

"Your Yellow makes you Peter Pan with brains," he continued. "Yellows have a child-like energy and are very sensitive. As a Yellow, you are here to bring joy to others – remind people that things can be done with a little more light-heartedness, playfulness, and fun. You also love nature and need to move your body a lot. If you don't, your energy gets stuck and you get grumpy. And if you don't take time for yourself, you get a sore throat or the flu."

He continued describing in detail what I had experienced many times throughout my life. "And Tans like to structure things. They are the engineers of our world. You have the ability to break complex things down and create structure," describing an ability that I could see weaving throughout my entire life. Then, he launched into describing the relationship with Jeanine, outlining specifically which moments we would be happy and where we would get into conflicts, down to the very details of how she behaved in specific situations: "She drives you up the tree when she continues discussing problems while you just want to shut off the light and go to sleep – and when she constantly changes things around at the last minute: your travel plans or your appointments." *Holy shit. How can he possibly know this without having been in the room with us?* He knew those exact situations that had driven me crazy, many times. He even told me how my parents' relationship was working and in which situations they would run into a conflict. And that even though they had a conflict, they would rarely speak about it. He described the areas my mum, my dad, and my siblings had difficulty understanding or relating to me, and where our relationships flourished, even though he had never seen them or heard anything about them.

As he continued, seemingly without taking a breath, I slowly felt my worldview crumble. I had been brought up with a pragmatic view of the world, believing that if I just got a good education, worked hard, landed a good job by being responsible, pragmatic, smart, and getting things done, life would turn out fine. And here was someone who pierced right through my construct, laying out why my approach had caused frustration in my life, and who I was here to *be* during this lifetime instead. *Can he really see all this? If he can, what else is "out there" that I don't have a clue about? This guy is describing my entire life to a T. Even my family doesn't understand me this well after decades of knowing each other.* But more profoundly than that, I realized something else was happening at that moment. Rob saw my authenticity. It felt like he looked directly into my soul. In fact, I noticed that, for the first time in my life at the age of thirty-three, I was being seen for who I was: my authentic personality with all its facets. A personality that even *I* had never fully seen. Without any judgment, he outlined the entire playbook of my world as though he had personally designed it. It seemed that all the whens and ifs and shoulds and musts, which had consumed so much time and energy, had been washed away, and, as a consequence, a surge of vitality was released. I resonated so deeply with how he described me that I had no doubt that this was the personality that wanted to be expressed during my lifetime.

The personality he described to me – my authentic personality – was profoundly different from how I had operated in my life so far, although I always had a subtle feeling, just like a barely audible voice, that what Rob described to me was how I *wanted* to live. However, the way I was raised, the way I was educated, the way my organizations operated, the way I thought I *should* behave had overshadowed that subtle feeling for so long I had dismissed that way of living as unrealistic. As a matter of fact, I realized that throughout my life, I had been educated *out* of my authenticity; and as a result, I didn't even know what my authentic personality was anymore. As I listened to Rob's words, it was as though a thick layer of fog lifted and made many facets of my life visible that had been out of reach before. As he described my authenticity, this subtle feeling of who I was really here to *be* expanded and allowed my energy to flow freely and unencumbered.

When he concluded, it felt like only forty minutes had passed. When I looked at my watch, Rob had in fact spoken for more than two hours. And I had barely said a word. When I stood up – *still* speechless – Rob gave me his big teddy bear hug and sent me staggering on my way. As I walked back along Carmel's shoreline to the house we had rented, I thought, *To truly see a person is the biggest gift we can give to anyone.* By seeing my authenticity, Rob gave me permission to be myself. It felt as though my soul had been yearning to live the way he described for a long time and finally a doorway was flung open. And there was nothing holding back this different way of living and being. As I looked out on the Pacific Ocean, I had the confidence – even the deep knowing – that living this authenticity would be the only way to live a truly fulfilled and successful life.

Your Authenticity: The Foundation
for Real Success

When you ask people whether they believe themselves to be authentic, most will confidently nod their head. As a matter of fact, I haven't met anyone who responded that they're inauthentic. I thought that I was being authentic before I met with Rob. I was *being myself* as much as I was able to. Yet after Rob revealed a deeper insight of who I was here to *be*, I realized that for most of my life I was being myself from a distorted viewpoint. After years of cultural and family conditioning, a good education in Germany and England, topped off with a master's degree in engineering, I didn't even know who I was. So how could I *be myself*? The best I could do – the best that most of us can do – is to be who we think we are.

But what if who we think we are isn't the truth?

What if there's a completely different level of authenticity and *being-ness* that we can access, where our daily challenges stop bothering us, where frustration and the search for meaning dissolves? Most of us feel this must be possible. It's likely that you've had glimpses of this deeper beingness: when you were immersed in nature or listened to a beautiful piece of music, felt connected to a loved one, meditated during a yoga retreat, or when you felt inspired by your work. In these moments of connection and flow, we live our authenticity – we expand into our beingness, and all the doing, planning, scheduling, and wanting subsides. For a moment in time, we live by the new success model. We feel complete. There's nothing to do, and nothing's missing. How can we expand this state of being in our daily lives?

The journey to authenticity is not only your personal one. It is our common journey we share as humans: to discover who we're here to *Be* during this lifetime. That discovery is calling us every time we feel frustrated or over-worked, when we wonder about our purpose, and even when we hold a grudge toward a family member or coworker. In those moments, our soul is nudging us to explore what's missing and how we can manifest more fully in the world. Whether we're listening to the call today or ten years from now doesn't matter. Our soul will continue to nudge us to discover who we're here to Be, always seeking to expand. When we end up sitting across from someone like Rob with his unique ability to deeply see into our Being and reflect our authenticity back to us, it is as though a veil is lifted and we're able to see, crystal clear, what we've been looking for all along. Unfortunately, the way we're raised, educated, or cultured at work doesn't support this discovery. Most of us never learned what our authenticity really is.

When you spend time with a baby, you get a glimpse. She isn't manipulating life. When she's happy, she smiles; when she's sad or hungry, she cries. Any emotion, whether anger, happiness, or sadness, flows right through her body, without resistance, stories, accusations, or judgments about the world or the people around her. Once the emotion has passed through her, she's back to being her happy self – experiencing the wonder of the world around her moment by moment. And all the while, you can't take your eyes off of the little thing because there's something so powerful about being authentic that you just want to keep looking. But then, a few years later, after mum or dad scolded her for spilling the spinach on the carpet, she quickly learns she needs to be nice if she wants to get love from her parents. At first, this doesn't feel quite right, but she has seen her mum displaying the same behavior, so it must be safe to adopt. In school, the same pattern gets reinforced when she realizes that in order to avoid judgment, she must get good grades. Her young brain, building neural pathways from scratch, cannot help but sponge up the behaviors, conditioning, and fears of her surroundings, parents, family, and teachers. By age six, she's using the same words her parents are using, displaying compatible traits in relationships with other kids on the playground. The Jesuits had it figured out when they said, "Give us a child before seven and we'll have them for life."

At age thirty-five, when she's sitting across from her boss for her annual appraisal, the same mechanism repeats itself: if she's good enough for the company, she'll get her bonus, if not, she'll get the pink slip. Rarely on our lifelong journey are we encouraged to discover who we're here to be. Our school teachers, managers, and even our parents are more interested in having you behave in a way that fits *their* image of the world – both to protect you and not to challenge their worldview. In your own life, when you expect your colleagues to be more engaged or your children more focused, do you see them for who they are or for who you want them to be? As a result, from an early age, we develop a conditioned personality (see diagram).

What We Strive Towards

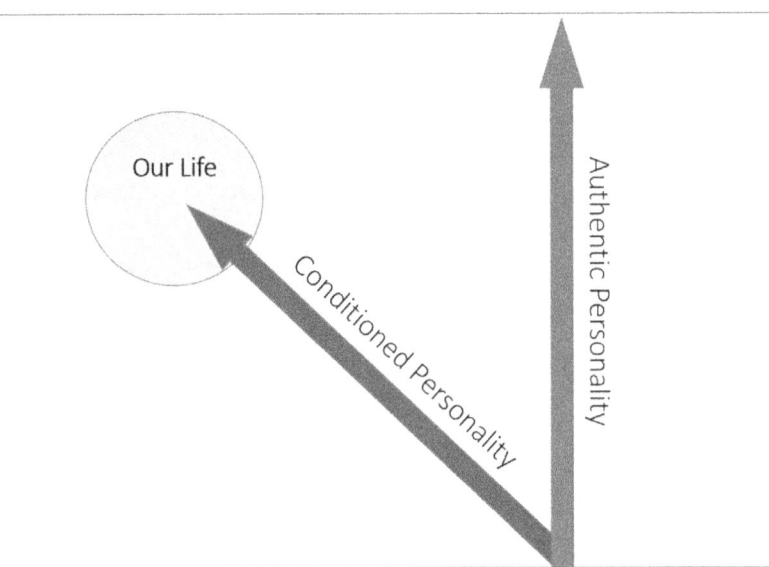

Graphic 2: Our authentic and conditioned personality

With our authentic personality slowly fading into the background, clouded by all the expectations and beliefs we learn over time, we establish ourselves out there in left field trying to make it while at the same time wondering why it doesn't feel quite right. This is our authenticity calling. A part of us wants to return to being authentic (the arrow pointing straight up). We intuitively feel that this would feel like "coming home" where we can be truly ourselves, live in the flow, and in alignment with our soul.

But we've built our entire life out there with our conditioned personality. For years, often decades, we've invested time, money, and energy to become an accountant or in my case a venture capitalist. Maybe you've done so well that you're now a director or VP of a global company. "How can we throw all that we've built to the curb and pursue something that we're not even clear what it looks like, whether it works, or whether it can sustain us," we ask ourselves. In addition, your friends, spouse, and boss have learned how you behave. It seems business as usual is somehow working for them. So, why is it not working for you? Also, you know that they like you the way you are – out there in left field – and they would wonder what's gotten into you if you suddenly changed. Deep down, you know that being fully yourself could upset your life. And yet, you still feel that pull.

The gap between who you're here to Be, your authentic personality, and your conditioned personality out there in left field has a name. It's called pain. Some of us feel this pain as a disease in the body, others as frustration, stress, resignation, anger, depression, or, in my own case, despair. When we feel this pain, all we want is for it to go away, for life to return to normal, without realizing that these exact feelings and many of our physical symptoms are the doorway leading us back to our authenticity.

Closing the Gap: Be Who You're Here to Be

Most people are taught that it's not good to show anger, frustration, or resignation. We believe others will judge us or see us as a failure if we haven't figured life out. And if that wasn't enough, we know that nobody wants to spend time with us if we're angry or frustrated. Meanwhile, these "negative" feelings are perfect indicators that we're not on our authentic path – that we need to change something if we want to reclaim our authentic power. Our feelings are street signs of the soul, ultimately directing us toward more fulfillment, purpose, happiness, and self-expression.

When you're stuck in the office at ten o'clock at night, frustrated and overwhelmed by all of the things you still need to complete, there's an opportunity right there and then to change your life. Instead of pushing your emotions to the side, rolling up your sleeves with a deep sigh, and digging into the pile of work, you can create a moment of grace and simply become aware of your frustration. To *be* present with your emotion, without the need to do anything about it. When you're able to simply *be* with the situation, without doing anything to fix it, you'll sense a richness and aliveness. Just like a baby feeling sadness or frustration, you're present to what's alive inside. You're *with* the emotion, not fighting it or ignoring it. This feeling of richness and aliveness in the moment, whether it's connected to happiness or frustration, love or fear, is a moment of authenticity. There's no need to manipulate the situation, defend yourself, convince anyone, look good, or be right. You're simply Being with what is.

That's different from what people commonly think authenticity means. Most agree that it's inauthentic when people act artificially nice or when their actions don't reflect what they're thinking and feeling. The stereotypical politician or sales person. Others think that a person is authentic when they speak what's on their mind. Without any political preference in mind, Donald Trump is an example of this misconception. His outspoken behaviors as a person are far from authentic because he broadcasts his unfiltered opinions and emotions into the world, projecting his judgments, anger, or blame onto others around him. When we're not present with our emotions and taking full responsibility and accountability for them, broadcasting our judgments and opinions is exactly the same as holding back and being artificially nice. Either way, we're not fully present with the situation at hand and what's going on inside of us. Instead, we try to influence the situation or the people around us with our words and actions.

When we pretend to be something or someone that we're not, we're inauthentic. That's a no-brainer. But every time we pretend without knowing that we do so, it is also inauthentic. It's inauthentic when we show up in a team meeting pretending that everything's fine when in fact we're overworked and frustrated about our boss; when we pretend that we've got it all figured out in life when in fact we're wondering what on earth our purpose is, or when we pretend that we have a five-step program to happiness when in fact we're just hoping that this message will make people buy our stuff. Every time we show up in the world as though everything is okay, when in fact we don't feel that way, we sacrifice our authenticity. We revert to the behavioral Model of Dominance & Subservience, not present and at peace with the situation in front of us and instead attempting to influence the situation with our actions. From this "out-of-power" position, we always expend energy and create stress for ourselves or the people around us. After being trained and behaving in this manner for decades, we wonder why we feel tired or exhausted.

The more we're able to remove the veil that's clouding our authenticity, the less we feel we need to pay attention to, influence, or manipulate the situations around us, and the more liberated we become. When you uncover your authenticity, whether through an experience like the one I had with Rob, through personality assessments, or through other insights that reveal a deeper understanding of your authentic personality, you'll access a completely different level of energy and possibility *which you didn't even know existed* – for yourself, your relationships, and your team. Like Jeanine, you'll jump with energy and zest when before you didn't even think that was possible. Whenever you grow in your authenticity, you access a greater level of empowerment, energy, and well-being.

Authenticity Is Effortless – And It Takes Work

There are two essential elements for expanding into your authentic power: personal growth and growing up. Personal growth develops a deeper understanding of who you are here to *be*; growing up prevents you from flying off the handle when things don't go your way, building your awareness and capacity to remain centered in emotional situations.

Personal Growth

When you ask a person whether they think they're authentic, no matter if they're fifteen, twenty-five, or fifty, they'll usually say yes. We see our level of authenticity through our own lens of awareness, so of course we think we're authentic. Most likely, though, your understanding of your authenticity changes substantially over time. At fifty, you might arrive at the realization that you didn't even know what being authentic meant when you were twenty. This makes authenticity a tricky business because there's no obvious image or destination we can see or aspire toward from our current point of view. Expanding into our authenticity isn't something we do; it is an inner process – an ever-expanding awareness of who we are in the present moment. The invisible guardrails, which guide us in this process, are all around us. Every day, our world mirrors back to us whether we're authentic or inauthentic – when we feel in the flow with our work, connect deeply to the person in front of us, or when we feel dissatisfied with our job – offering us an opportunity to explore what choices we've made and which adjustments are necessary if we want to expand further into our authenticity.

Events such as my meeting with Rob in Carmel, moments of enlightenment, or, if your soul prefers, a near-death experience can give us a rocket boost in understanding our authenticity, laying open those facets of our unique personality that have so far been invisible to us. When I learned from Rob that I was a Violet Yellow with Tan, it instantly revealed parts of me which I had sensed for decades but didn't allow myself to express. After the meeting, the veil was lifted and these parts of my authentic personality became accessible to me. I gained the clarity of what it meant to show up as a "violet" in the world and – even more importantly – the courage to express that part of my personality.

Even a disease diagnosis can reveal a deeper understanding of who you're here to be. Dr. Gabor Maté, the physician and best-selling author in the field of trauma, was diagnosed with ADD in his fifties. Instead of seeing it as an impairment, the diagnosis was liberating for him. He shared in a workshop in 2012 that he had always felt incomplete, even flawed; and although he had always wanted to write a book, he felt that he always had to do other things to feel complete. After his diagnosis, the puzzle pieces fell into place. It became apparent why he felt the way he did throughout his life. There wasn't anything wrong with him – he just had ADD. Deepening the understanding of his authentic personality liberated him to stop what he was previously chasing, pick up the pen, and write three best-selling books.

Being authentic doesn't require effort. Oddly enough, when we are in our authentic power, we can even achieve more by doing less, a ray of sunlight in our busy world. Consider Dr. Martin Luther King Jr. He certainly got things done in the real world; but when listening to Dr. King speak you don't hear a need to manipulate, defend, politicize, or convince his audience, nor does he denounce others. His power lies in his authenticity, to simply express his truth and his bold dream, taking a stand for racial justice without being attached to recognition, selling a program, manipulating, judging the people around him, or getting something. Observe any person who you admire for their authenticity – whether it's Oprah, Mother Teresa, Gandhi, or Nelson Mandela – and you see that authenticity doesn't require effort. These individuals aren't *doing* authentic, they're *being* authentic. In those moments of authenticity, they're in a different state of mind, so aligned and centered in who they are here to *be* that there's no need for them to pretend to be someone else or to get somewhere. Life doesn't happen by them, it flows through them. Any forcefulness or manipulation of inauthentic behaviors pales in comparison to the power of authenticity.

We've all experienced this level of authentic power in our own life. When you're in the flow, brainstorming with colleagues at work, playing with your children, playing an instrument, or simply being present with what's in front of you, you're untethered from the outcome or the need to do anything or to get somewhere. You're not rushing to the final chord; you're present with each note as it comes, fulfilled being right "here" instead of "there." Consider how it would feel to show up that way all the time, bringing your unique personality into the room, able to respond to what's in front of you right there and then, without the need to get some place or manipulate other people. Are you able to sense the ease, the peace, and maybe your power and centeredness when you show up that way?

Growing Up

Growing up takes work. Let's say you made an appointment with your friend and he shows up half an hour late. This is not the first time this has happened, so you become aggravated. As more time passes, you feel angry. If, when your friend arrives, you accuse him of being late, telling him that it has happened many times before and that you've had enough, you're *not* being authentic. It's a misconception that speaking what's on our mind is authentic. It's not because you're not taking responsibility for your emotions. You're making your friend responsible for your emotions.

Growing into your authenticity is an internal process requiring awareness and responsibility for your own emotions. The story that's unfolding between your ears when your friend shows up late is yours. Why? Because someone else who experiences the exact same situations could sit right next to you and *not* feel anger or frustration and feel gratitude for a little extra time for herself instead. When we feel anger, frustration, disrespect, or any other negative emotions, our conditioned response is to look for someone to blame or to make outside circumstances responsible for our feelings. We point the finger and accuse others of their wrongdoing, or we try to be right. This is not authentic power but domination and control. We use the Model of Dominance & Subservience to get what we want – in our example, to have your friend show up on time. When the Model of Dominance & Subservience takes over our thoughts and actions, we're not authentic. We behave from a distorted reality that's made up between our ears.

How can we behave, instead? Rather than judging your friend or holding a passive aggression toward her for showing up late, we can become conscious of and accountable for our own anger. We can become curious about what we've been missing in the relationship. On the surface, we want our friend to be on time. But on a deeper level we might want respect, feeling valued, or need to be able to count on her. When you become aware of your emotions and what you're missing, you open the door to remaining in your authentic power even in challenging situations because only when you're aware of your emotions are you able to speak to what's alive inside of you. You could say, for example, "When I see you arrive thirty minutes after our agreed time, I feel really angry – even furious. To maintain respect in our relationship, I need our meetings to be on time. What's needed to make that happen?" This way, you own your emotions *and* you're setting clear boundaries for your relationship without accusing your friend or spilling your unfiltered emotions. Since your friend isn't judged or accused by what you say, she's more willing to listen.

Is this easy to practice in our daily lives, especially when we're emotionally triggered? No, it's not. For decades, we've been conditioned to either judge the other or to shut up and swallow our emotions. Even media headlines reinforce the need for judgment: who's to blame? We might not even be used to feeling our emotions, let alone taking full responsibility for them. I literally had to relearn feeling my emotions. But when we're able to relearn to express our emotions in an authentic way, we create connection and transparency rather than conflict and separation. As you reveal to your friend what's going on inside of you, she's able to "see into you." You develop "into-me-see." Intimacy. The basis for trust and connection. By being authentic, we can turn negative emotions and events into an opportunity to create more connection, closeness, and trust.

Your Authentic Power: The 1ˢᵗ Fundamental Shift

In our pressure-cooker world, is it realistic to be fully authentic? Whether we're at home or at work, we have to meet other people's expectations:

our boss's expectation to increase sales, Wall Street's quarterly earnings expectations, our parent's expectation to be a good child, or the many expectations we have for our own life. Even our legal system is designed to meet other people's expectations. When a public company doesn't meet its financial forecasts, plaintiff lawyers roll up their sleeves and sue the company's officers. For many of us, the fear of what's going to happen if we don't meet other people's expectations has become a steadfast companion, wondering during the day whether our work performance is good enough, or when we wake up in the middle of the night, adding items to our never-ending to-do list.

The new success model appears simple and trivial, but how many people do you know that live by this model? How many of today's organizations operate by this model? And as you wonder whether it's possible or even smart to be fully authentic in the real world, you may come to the conclusion that living by the BE – DO – HAVE model isn't realistic at all because, if it was, you would have done it a long time ago.

If you want to install the new success model in your life or business, the first step is to understand that this journey starts with yourself. Transforming your success and your relationships or building better workplaces doesn't start by changing outside circumstances – a job change, hiring different employees, or changing your spouse. It doesn't start by developing new strategies or change initiatives. By changing outside circumstances, we might be able to improve a situation, but because this approach usually originates from the same system of thinking – the same level of consciousness – we can't expect true transformation. Transformation requires a different level of consciousness, which starts with self-awareness.

This approach is contrary to what we're used to. When I work with leaders, most of them get very excited about what's possible for their company, but shortly after, they want to roll up their sleeves and get to work. "That sounds great. What should I *do* differently, now?" they ask. We're addicted to changing outside circumstances – to shaping the world around us so we can get what we think we need. *Voilà*, the old success model. Most of our energy and time is fixated on creating outer peace: success at work, making enough money, a happy relationship, a nice car, or recognition from others. Browse through your emails and look at how many people are promising happiness if you just bought their stuff or did this one thing: if you buy this new dress, this magic program for health and happiness, things will be better. Our addiction to *doing* is even more pronounced in the work world. After we've met our sales target, our boss says, "Well done," then immediately outlines the expected increase for next year. How many things do you do, day-in and day-out, to fix outside issues and concerns? "If I get the next promotion, then I'll be where I want to be." "If I make a couple of million dollars, then I'll be fine." In those moments when we're focused on changing outside circumstances or trying to reach a destination, we're not expressing our authentic power. We're not *being with* the situation that's right in front of us anymore. Instead, we're attempting to manipulate the world around us to get to where we want to be. Let's face it, for the vast majority, it's not working well.

When you observe individuals who are in the flow – a scientist who is so engrossed in her work that she forgets time and space or a dancer who is fully present with his movements – these individuals don't seem to be "working" in that moment. They're expressing themselves in the present moment and expanding their potential to the best of their abilities. Remember from the first chapter, when you listen to Richard Branson, the founder of the Virgin groups of companies, speak at a conference, watch violinist Joshua Bell, or the jazz trumpeter Miles Davis play, you witness flow. In those moments, they're not attempting to influence an outcome, trying to get somewhere. There's a calmness, a centeredness, and presence that differs vastly from much of the *doing* we see in organizations. This state of *Being* is not only nice to have. According to research, it literally allows us to access a higher level of performance.

Richard Davidson and his neuroscience team at the University of Wisconsin researched the brain patterns of monks, discovering that in states of meditation – a deep state of Beingness – they showed substantially elevated gamma oscillations, the brainwave frequency that occurs when multiple brain regions are activated in harmony, such as moments of insights. For most of us, gamma states only last for a few seconds at most. The monks were able to reach this state for minutes at a time, and it often endured even in their day-to-day activities, giving the brain the feeling of being in peak mental and physical condition – to be in the "zone." In their research, neuroscientists have found that people with high levels of gamma frequency are exceptionally intelligent, compassionate, focused, calm, and peaceful. How can we reach that level of performance, presence, and authenticity – this state of Being where life flows through us?

The Dalai Lama states in *The Art of Happiness* that when we experience a conflict in life, we're missing one insight that would change the situation. In meeting with Rob, the one insight that helped me expand into my authenticity was the realization that there's a higher purpose to our lives, that we're not alone in the world, there's a higher source and guidance. When Rob saw my authentic personality, describing my parents, friends, and coworkers and their personalities to a T, I had to ask myself some fundamental questions. If someone has the ability to access all of this information from a leather chair in Carmel, what are the implications for our lives, for the way we relate to each other, or the way we conduct business? What are the implications if all of us have a unique personality – our unique authenticity – that someone can "see" without knowing one iota about you?

It implies that you're not just one of eight billion separate individuals trying to make it in this world; instead, we're interconnected on some deeper level, part of a bigger picture – like a water drop that's part of a wave, which in turn is part of an ocean. In his ability to "know" me, Rob is just another part of the same ocean, connected with me, with you, and every other water drop if he chooses to. When you hold this bigger picture in your mind, even the most challenging events in your life, such as losing a loved one or getting fired, obtain a different meaning. Everything changes when you live with this expanded consciousness. Not only can we relax a bit, we also don't need to revert to the Model of Dominance & Subservience to get things done because we know that there's a deeper purpose for the present situation.

Sometimes I ask people before a speech, "How many of you have experienced devastating life situations – the loss of a loved one, a divorce, financial hardship, or getting fired?" Everyone raises their hand. Then I ask how many in the audience feel that after some time had passed, the difficult event helped them grow as a person, in their career, or their life. Everyone's hand goes up.

What if you knew – not only in your head, but deep down in your body – that you're here to express your authenticity, that there's a bigger picture to the unfolding of your life, and if you didn't express who you are here to be, something would be lost in the world? If you knew this was the truth, how would you live? How would your interactions with others change? In your workplace, how would the way people work together change if we saw each other's unique personalities and supported each other in our higher purpose?

Rick Ridgeway, a mountaineer and former vice president at the outdoor clothing manufacturer Patagonia, explained how a sense of interconnectedness translates into the company's business meetings. Since 1983,

Patagonia has run on-site childcare centers in their Ventura headquarters. Some of the playgrounds are located right between office buildings, exposing several of their conference rooms to the steady background noise of children playing. Ridgewood explains: "The meetings we hold in the conference rooms where we hear our children are very different from meetings where we don't hear children playing in the background. People are much more respectful of each other, more open and transparent, and there's much better collaboration." Just transitioning from the self as a point of focus to a broader feeling of connectedness resulted in completely different meetings.

Is this different reality true? Are we really interconnected and part of something bigger, which reaches far beyond our personal reality? Ultimately, this is your choice. There's no final proof either way – whether we're just here on our own striving for ourselves and maybe for our family or whether there's a different reality that we can step into, in which there's a higher guidance and purpose for our lives.

For people who have had near-death experiences, it seems that there's more evidence that we're part of something larger and less evidence that we are all by ourselves. My dear friend Jessica, who broke countless bones and was later declared clinically dead after a severe car accident, healed herself in only a few weeks after "coming back to life." But not only did her body heal, to the amazement of the doctors, she also "saw" (when she was clinically dead) that her then-husband had had an affair with another woman. She even knew exactly when it happened and with whom. To the surprise of her husband, she revealed what she saw and fired him as her husband when he came to visit her in the hospital. From Harvard-trained neuroscientist Eben Alexander to best-selling author Anita Moorjani, most of the individuals who have been proclaimed clinically dead and returned to life report strikingly similar experiences and in many cases created inexplicable physical healing shortly after they returned to our reality. One single thought – whether we're all separate individuals or we're interconnected – can create fundamentally different outcomes in your life. This bigger picture of our authenticity, of who we're here to Be, can influence our well-being, our peace of mind, the quality of our relationships, and the way we create success.

This chapter has provided you with a glimpse of your authenticity – the Being part of the new success model and the foundation for creating more wholesome success. But ultimately, if we want to create anything in our world, sitting in an expanded state of being isn't enough. There's a point where we need to roll up our sleeves and get to work: the Doing part of the new success model.

Activity: Authenticity and Being

Unfortunately, I can't give you the same experience that I had when sitting across from Rob. If you'd like to learn more, feel free to reach out to our team at the Conscious Business Institute or dive deeper with the recommended material in the resources section.

To give you an idea about your authentic personality, we invite you take our CBI Personality Color Assessment included in the Plan BE Online Course in the resources section or at https://cbipersonalityassessment.consciousbusinessinstitute.com.

CHAPTER 5

Your Magic: Where Work Becomes Flow

"Everyone is a genius. But if you judge a fish by its ability to climb a tree, it will live its whole life believing that it is stupid."

– Albert Einstein

The second element of the BE – DO – HAVE success model is to *do what your gifts inspire*. It doesn't state to do more or work harder, but to live out those unique gifts we're here to express. I call these our Magic. It is in those moments when we're able to express our Magic that work becomes effortless. Even when a client calls you at ten o'clock at night, it doesn't feel like work if you get to express your Magic.

Anna, a director for a global automotive company, was managing a team of fifty people when she was invited by her boss to participate in a nine-month leadership program. As part of the program, every participant received a series of coaching sessions, which gave me the opportunity to work with Anna as her coach. During our first meeting, Anna laid out her personal and professional circumstances to me, summarizing that she felt she was doing quite well overall. She felt confident and happy in her job, she mothered two teenage children, which weren't causing too much trouble, and she had a well-functioning relationship with her husband. Everything seemed to be going well for Anna.

When I asked her what kind of life she would create if I were a fairy who could grant her wishes, she leaned back, turned inward, and reflected. After a while, her eyes focused back on me and she said, "I know I'm doing quite well overall. But when you ask me that question, I feel there's a completely different way I'd live. More in tune with myself and with the people around me, where I would make the contribution in the world I'm here to make."

I asked whether she would be interested in an assessment that would help her discover her Magic – the unique contribution she's here to bring into the world. Her eyes opened wider and she agreed. Once she had completed the assessment, it turned out that her unique talent was what I call "Phoenix Magic" – the ability to guide people through change processes and tricky transitions, which often require the old ways to die before the new can emerge. While many people try maintaining the status quo, for Anna change was second nature. After she learned about her Magic she agreed wholeheartedly, explaining that she had seen many times in her company that most people try to avoid change. "While they're trying to hold on to our existing products or people, trying to keep things safe," she said, "I love when things are being transformed, and I love leading others through the process of change." Where others freaked out, Anna thrived. Whenever there was change, she became as calm and centered as the eye of a storm.

Even in her personal life she was the one who initiated changes, suggesting to her children and partner to try new things, visit new places, or shake up the daily family routines. When she shared her experiences around transformation, it became crystal clear that she was intimately familiar with the natural cycle of birth, growth, maturation, decay, and death. "Most people I know want to hold on to the things they've created," she explained. "For me, I know exactly when to let go and that the death of one thing is the birth of a new opportunity." It was as though the understanding of this natural cycle was deeply programmed into her.

At the end of our session, I asked her to make a list of how much she has been able to use her Magic at work. In our next meeting, she reported that she wasn't having many opportunities at all in her current position to facilitate the level of change that would excite her. Most of her daily work was spent on regular management tasks – managing goals, providing vision and expectations, and keeping the team inspired and on track. After we examined some of the situations where she had actually been able to live her Magic, she realized that those were the times when she was at her best – feeling in the flow, being herself, and finding appreciation from others for what she brought to the table.

As our time together progressed, she clarified how her Magic exactly worked. She started owning it. She scheduled meetings with HR managers and other leaders in her company, sharing her unique talent and her desire to lead big change projects. Within a year, she was offered the Managing Director position for Australia. The organization needed a large-scale transformation, and she was the right person for the job.

Get More by Doing Less

When we express our unique Magic, we're not just enjoying work a bit more. It's as though we're stepping into another reality of work, in which we can thrive professionally and financially without needing to work harder. We're stepping out of Newton's linear reality of do-more-to-get-more and entering Einstein's quantum reality of get-more-by-doing-less. Most of us know how it feels when we express our Magic. We experience a sense of resonance where work stops being work. We become the vessel through which our Magic gets expressed in the world. Some feel it when they present or perform for others, others when they give advice to a friend, support a colleague, or brainstorm a new idea. And yet, most of us are not consciously aware of exactly what our unique gift is or how we can contribute it fully in the world.

To discover your Magic, ask yourself what topic people have repeatedly approached you for help with. What have they asked you? When I posed this question to myself, I realized that people have approached me to get a better understanding of how we tick as humans and how to better deal with personal or professional challenges. Upon closer examination, I realized that there was a common question people were asking: "What am I or what are we doing that causes these issues in my life, in our company, or in the world?" At first, this common thread wasn't obvious to me, nor did I have any idea why people approached me with their questions. It seemed that I was oozing out this energy without saying it, and others recognized and trusted it. On a flight to Zurich, during a due diligence phase for an investment, one of my suit-and-tie venture capital colleagues turned to me and asked: "Peter, you always seem so easygoing and balanced with work [not true from my perspective, by the way]. Everyone else is hustling and striving for more, and so am I. It seems that you just know things will be okay. How do you do that?"

To look at the questions people have asked me has been a powerful exercise, and I encourage you to do the same.

Once you find the pattern that people approach you for, you'll realize that you've expressed your Magic all along, countless times since you've been a teenager or even earlier. Maybe if you had a good leader that recognized your talent, you were even offered a position that allowed you to express your Magic at work. But since you've expressed it for so long, it's likely that it has become second nature to you, so much so that you might not even notice when you express it, let alone the value it brings to others. But the opposite is the truth: your Magic is your biggest asset, and you should get paid handsomely for it.

Bridging Money and Meaning

In 2009, Olivier Kohler, a Swiss-born Silicon Valley manager, was meeting with top-level executives of the networking giant Cisco Systems. Cisco leaders knew that the digital world was coming, demanding companies to be flexible and fast, and that their organization had grown fatter and slower with hierarchies, policies, and administrative processes over the years. Olivier was brought in to help make Cisco nimbler and more prepared for the future. He had previously been the global head and general manager for Hewlett-Packard's Enterprise Strategic Alliances organization, making a name for himself cleaning the organization up like no one else. Cisco leaders wanted the same for their company.

During the meeting, Olivier stated clearly that his conditions would be to join in a C-level position, and that he needed completely free rein on how he would operate. Then he added, "I will shake things up, and I'm not sure whether you're ready for this." They were not. The meeting concluded, and everyone went their separate ways.

Nine months later, Olivier received a call. The man at the other end of the line said that Cisco was now ready and asked whether he would be open to meeting again. Shortly after, Olivier joined the Cisco team as a chief administrative officer and senior vice president, rolling up his sleeves, ready to get to work.

When I spoke with Olivier during an executive briefing session at the Cisco Systems headquarters in 2012, he said: "This is what I do. I come into organizations and I clean up – get rid of all the inefficiencies and administrative fat. I've done it at Hewlett-Packard, and now I'm doing it at Cisco." Still today Olivier is expressing his Magic. At the time I'm writing these lines, he's working his Magic as the COO of Trinet. And if you wonder whether expressing one's Magic can pay the bills, look up the company's financial information. Olivier earned more than $4 million in 2021.

Unfortunately, most people aren't fully aware of their Magic. As long as we're not consciously bringing our Magic into the world, it can't grow into its full power. We won't be able to live our potential as long as we're acting in response to outside requests rather than steering our own journey. But most importantly, if we're not conscious of our Magic, we'll never appreciate the value it can bring to the people we touch. To live in the flow, like Olivier expressing his Magic, we must first recognize its power. We must "own" the beauty of our Magic and the positive impact we're able to create with it. Once we do that – with humbleness rather than ego or entitlement, like an artist practicing his art – we're able to access the full power and value of our Magic.

Making a Living with Your Magic

You might already have a sense of how expressing your Magic helps you create more ease in your life. Maybe it has already become clear why expressing your unique talent is essential if you want to get out of the rat race and live by the BE – DO – HAVE success model. Still, many people wonder whether bringing their Magic is enough to create success in our current-day work world or if there will always be some struggle to cope with our daily challenges. When we have to meet a project deadline, is it realistic to become like an island of ease and authenticity in an ocean of people that are running around to meet goals, agendas, and timelines? It certainly takes time and focus to build this island, but once you do, you'll find that it's not only possible, but it's the only way to thrive.

A turning point that helped me build this island for myself was a conversation with one of my mentors, Jennie, in February of 2002. During the phone call, she revealed my Magic to me. We had scheduled regular check-ins during my transition toward more fulfilling and satisfying work. Jennie had been a turnaround manager in Silicon Valley when she first noticed that she was receiving messages from several Native American elders during her meditations. During the years following the first messages, she tried to bridge her fast-paced tech life with strengthening her newly found spiritual abilities. Eventually, she realized that it would be impossible to consolidate both, and, after she made the decision to quit the nine-to-five world, the nuggets of wisdom she received became more expansive and clearer. Her Native American guides started feeding information to her about how we tick as human beings and what we can do to improve our human condition – a powerful body of wisdom from the other side. One chapter of the information she received was about our unique Magic.

When I spoke with her from my cushy leather chair in the office on that cold February evening, she halted our conversation midway and said that she wanted to tell me about my Magic. I became curious, wondering whether her insights would help me get more clarity for my path forward.

"You're an Illumination Magic," she continued. I sat forward in my chair, eager to hear more. "You're designed to observe and explain to people the problem with our current structure of thinking and behaving. You see what's working and not working. You see how our current way of conducting business is flawed, and why it's not working for most people. As you describe this to people, your words provide insights to others that have the power to transform everything." In my mind, I started flipping through my rolodex of situations in which I felt in the flow: when people came to me for advice; when I was speaking at conferences about trends or business culture; and even the times when a single, deep personal conversation saved the night at an otherwise dull networking event.

As Jennie and I analyzed some of these situations together, I started to see that whenever I was using my Illumination Magic, I felt energized. There was never a time when I felt like a fish out of water. When I was expressing my Magic, I felt solid, centered, as though I had come home at last. But more importantly, I noticed that there was never a sense of scarcity in those moments. It was as though I left the three-dimensional world and entered a different reality in which I had access to a higher sense of knowing, where friction, resistance, or frustration didn't exist anymore, and to my relief, I didn't have any need to prove myself. In the moments when I expressed my Magic, I wasn't Doing. I was Being.

The more Jennie and I discussed examples of flow in my career, things in my brain started to click into place: a situation bubbled up in my mind when I was coaching a business client – a male executive in his late fifties. During the session, we had shifted away from speaking about his business and had dived deeply into topics that were close to his heart: his relationship to his wife and daughter and his dream to move to Hawaii where he wanted to work in a sector that would empower children. As I went into Illumination Magic mode and shared with my client what

I was observing, it was as though we both left time and space. There was a deep connection between us, as though our souls were speaking to each other. We felt love even though we were on the phone and had never met in person. The deeper I reflected, the more I realized how many times I had used my Magic and how powerful those particular times had been. Yet one part of the puzzle was still unclear to me: how to make a living with my Magic. How would I be able to create a career where I could just show up with my Magic?

That took time. And unless you already live your Magic today, it will likely take time for you as well. It will take time to understand how your exact Magic works as you replay those times in your mind when you expressed it and felt in the flow without even noticing it. After that comes an even trickier part: to "own" your Magic and embody that it is worth a lot even though it comes easily for you and you might have never considered charging a dime for it. This will be the moment when you "get" the dichotomy of success: that you can grow and expand your career by doing less.

After "owning" your Magic, your next step is to express it in a way that other people understand the impact you can make for them. Once you get to that point, you'll step out of the ordinary realm. You'll show up and speak in a way that other people simply trust you. Without even knowing why, they'll sense the inner alignment of who you are with what you do. You show up authentically, just like Anna when she was sharing her power as a changemaker and her managers trusted her – without consciously knowing why – to lead the Australian continent. Ultimately, you'll start shifting what you do on a daily basis to reflect more of your Magic. It might be within your organization or in other ways. This isn't something you'll need to push for, nor will you need to wonder about the right time to make big career changes. Instead, you'll find yourself growing into your new world organically, just like a tree knowing when it's time to blossom.

In my particular case, I didn't find enough ways to express my Magic within my existing job as a venture capitalist. Believe me, I tried. I wanted to make it fit. Instead, over the years, I've created my own playground: a business in which I can express my Illumination Magic in most of the things we do, from executive development programs and online courses to keynote speeches and leading the Conscious Business movement.

The more you embrace your Magic, the more doors and pathways will open before you. Your job is to remain aligned with who you're here to be. When you do, the universe will do its part to provide opportunities for you to express your Magic in the world. After you've expanded into the Being and Doing components of the new success model, let's now look at the final component: to Have what you seek to experience in life. Your Essences.

Reflection: Your Magic

The following questions help you become more familiar with your unique Magic. If you'd like to dive deeper and take an online assessment to discover your Magic, check out the Plan BE Online Course in the resource section at the end of the book.

1. What have people repeatedly approached you about throughout your life?

2. Why are they turning to you? What is their issue, and what do you leave them with? For example, this can

include concrete results, a deeper understanding of a situation, or feeling states they'd like to experience.

3. Assess whether providing this to others feels like work. Expressing your Magic should come easily to you and not feel like work.

4. Find situations in which you've expressed your Magic in a work environment. Assess how it felt and what the results were of expressing your Magic on others and what the outcomes have been.

5. Determine circumstances in our world in which the contribution of your Magic would be of great value. For example, the ability to heal conflicts would be of great value in war situations, couples divorcing each other, or legal fights between companies. Think outside the box until you viscerally feel the potential value of your Magic, no matter how grand or small the situation.

6. What's one step you can do to deepen your understanding of your Magic or express your Magic more powerfully?

CHAPTER 6

Essence:
From External Force
to Internal Power

"Life's a Feeling experience, not a Doing experience."
— Me

In 2004, I was asked to coach a wealthy investment banker from Stamford, Connecticut. Tom, my new client, was in his forties. Shortly before enrolling in our coaching program, he had quit his investment banking position in New York City and now he wanted a sounding board to discuss his next career steps.

We started biweekly conversations speaking about his career and the ins and outs of the finance sector, which I was familiar with through my venture capitalist background. Job decisions at Tom's seniority and pay rate aren't made lightly, so we discussed topics such as his positioning and listed companies that would be the best cultural fit for him. But after a few sessions, our conversations changed. After Tom started to trust me more, he opened up about his personal life, confessing to me that he felt miserable, frustrated, and under an enormous amount of pressure to bring home money. Here was a man who had it all, at least according to society's standards: a kick-ass wife, two children, a beautiful mansion in Connecticut, great schools for his children, and a lifestyle that only a few in the world will ever get to enjoy. And yet, he was miserable. "I don't know how I can keep doing this," he said. "Our standard of living is killing me. I need to net at least $35,000 per month to make it work – for the house, the schools, and to keep our circle of friends." In my head, I quickly calculated that, pre-tax, Tom had to bring at least $50,000 home every month. That wouldn't have been a stretch if he loved the investment banking world. But he didn't. He had maneuvered himself into a corner. He said he'd either have to lose the house and lifestyle or continue being miserable doing something he didn't love.

Tom is just one of millions who walk into their office each day because they want to maintain the standard of living they've created for themselves and their families. This is no coincidence. For centuries, most of us have been trained to focus our attention on creating or accumulating external, tangible things. The law degree, reaching a managing director position in a reputable company, buying a nice house, creating a family, and, of course, making money. The DO – ACCUMULATE – BECOME model makes it plain: accumulate more stuff or titles and you'll become something or someone.

Even the way we go about achieving all the external success metrics is through external means. We completely live our life through our five senses. We *see* what we want, we *hear* what others have, we *speak* to sell stuff, we stay away from things that don't *smell* good, and we use our *hands* – maybe feet if you're a soccer player – to get stuff done. It's even ingrained in our language when we tell others to "roll up your sleeves and get to work." If something doesn't work for us, doesn't taste or smell good, we try to change the situation through external means as well.

When we're upset with a coworker, we don't usually shift our mindset about the situation. We use words or actions to influence it, to tell them what we think or avoid them at the water cooler.

Look at a day in your own life. From dawn till dusk, your life is all about desires you'll experience through your senses: from the coffee, tea, or orange juice you desire for breakfast, the fancy car or dress you see someone with on your way to work, right to the last minutes of your day when you desire to read a book or watch the new episode of your favorite TV show. Some of us desire a beautiful relationship, a family, tenure as a professor, a promotion, or – the default choice for many – financial abundance.

Clearly, as we follow this model of success, we're barking up the wrong tree. If this model was working, every VP would be happier than their director, couples with children would be happier than those without, and people with more money would be happier than those with less. A look at happiness studies and the number of marriages ending in divorce makes it clear this model of success is broken.

We know that the promise to live a happy life once we have a job, house, family, fancy car, Prada purse, or boat isn't true. And yet, just like Tom, we keep doing the same thing, expecting different results. Most of us spend large amounts of our time and energy reaching for a destination, trying to get somewhere or get something. We drive to work every day and strive to get ahead for just a few more years, maybe because we need security and a decent health insurance for our family, or to reach the top of the food chain in the company, all the while thinking, *It's coming, it's coming – the time when things become easier, when we can finally relax.* If we're lucky, as the years pass, we realize that we've been climbing the wrong mountain all along; that life isn't about reaching a destination where we live on a golf course and wait for our children to bring the grandkids over. We realize that life is about experiencing each moment. The purpose is to grow, to expand into our authenticity, to have joy, and to be present with whatever is right in front of us on life's buffet, whether it's desire, happiness, frustration, love, or even pain.

Four Stages to Live Your Life

The way we live and create our lives can be grouped into four general stages, which each reflect our level of consciousness. These stages were developed by my dear friend Adam Hall, impact investor, shaman, and founder of the Genius Studio.

In stage one, we experience life as a victim. We're usually busy reacting to the circumstances around us. We point fingers, feel disempowered, and complain about our body, money, lack of time, other people, or the many other things that aren't right. Of course, most of us don't want to spend our days in victimhood, so our knee-jerk compensation is to become forceful. We clench our fists, accuse others, become angry, or judge other people's behaviors. In stage one, life happens *to you*.

Usually, people like to think they're beyond that stage. Considering that any frustration, outrage, or judgment points to a victim mindset, all of us could benefit from paying attention when we operate from this lack-based stage of consciousness. For me, personally, this reflection – and often painful realization – has become part of my daily routine.

In stage two, we manifest our own life. The book and movie *The Secret* helped millions of people move from stage one behavior to taking charge of their own life. In stage two, life happens *by you*. You're in the driver's seat and creating your reality. However, at this stage of consciousness, we usually still operate from a scarcity mindset, trying to fix a perception of lack in our lives. We're still manifesting stuff, trying to get more or become more – pushed by the desire to have more balance, a fulfilling relationship, a better job, or more money. At this stage, we're still driven by the DO – ACCUMULATE – BECOME success model.

If you're reading this book, it is likely that you feel pulled by the third stage, if not the fourth. Stage three transitions you to the BE – DO – HAVE success model. You become a vessel for your soul's expression. Your gifts, your talents, and your authentic personality are expressed through you – with a deep knowingness that life will unfold as it should. Rather than manifesting a better relationship, a better job, or more money so that you *Become* happy or fulfilled, you show up being fully yourself. You surrender to the flow of life. This doesn't mean you need to drop your intentions or goals. By golly – we're living in this incredible world of possibilities, so why not shoot for the stars? But is it possible to hold these intentions without being attached to an outcome? Rather than a salesman wanting to sell a car (stage two), imagine offering the car without any attachment to the outcome. If you prefer a more spiritual example, imagine Jesus sharing insights with his disciples. In stage two consciousness, he would try to convince them to join his movement. In stage three, words flow through him without attachment to the outcome. There's no one to convince, convert, or change. In stage three, life happens *through you*.

And lastly, in stage four, *you become life*. You experience oneness with everything around you. You know that you're a part of the whole. Just like a water drop is part of the wave or a sunray is an emanation of the sun, you know that you don't exist as a separate entity but that you're an expression of a greater beingness. Most people have experienced moments of oneness in one way or another: in nature, when dancing or listening to music, or during a meditation. In stage four, the illusion of separateness dissolves as you feel on a visceral level that you're connected to everything and everyone around you. At this stage, it becomes impossible to judge others, because you know that if you did, you'd judge yourself. It becomes impossible to conduct business in a way that's harmful to others or to our planet because you're so connected you feel the impact in your own body and psyche. Rumi describes this level of consciousness in his poem "A Great Wagon":

> Out beyond ideas of wrongdoing and rightdoing,
> there is a field. I'll meet you there.
>
> When the soul lies down in that grass,
> the world is too full to talk about.
> Ideas, language, even the phrase each other
> doesn't make any sense.

Essences: Moving from Stage Two to Stage Three

This book's focus is to shift our life paradigm from stage two to stage three – a place where life happens through you with an increased sense of ease, flow, and abundance. A way of life where we've realized that there's no destination to reach. Instead of striving to "become" someone or get some place, we're present with what's in front of us, whether it's a moment of unconditional love with your spouse or the death of a family member.

To live that way requires a fundamental shift in consciousness – from measuring our life's quality and success through external measures, such as our title, wealth, family, house, accumulations, accolades, or status symbols, to assessing it through inner means and qualities: through *Essences*.

Essences are our deepest drivers: the feeling states we have when we do something, reach a goal, or achieve a desired outcome in our life. Let's say your goal is to have ten million dollars in your bank account, a nice chunk of cash for most of us. What's motivating you to reach that goal isn't the money, it's the feeling state you associate with that amount of wealth: freedom, independence, peace of mind, or appreciation, for example. Essences are the driving force in life. It's not the money, the next career step, the house, or the beautiful relationship we're after – it's the feeling state we associate with these things. When you dream of a house by the beach, for example, what you really seek is the feeling states that you hope to experience when you are in that house and look out at the beach – a sense of achievement, freedom, happiness, or creativity.

Everything we do in life, every empowered decision we make, every action we take, we do to experience the Essences we desire. Every desire we pursue throughout the course of our day, from wanting to drink coffee or tea to watching our favorite TV show, is ultimately driven by Essences.

The distinction – whether we're striving for material outcomes and goals or the feeling states that ultimately drive those goals – is critical for our overall well-being and success. First, there's a good chance that we might never reach our material goals. We might never reach the pleasure of having ten million dollars in the bank, we might never get to sit in our own beach house overlooking the ocean. Meanwhile, for much of our life we chase a carrot, ultimately creating much of the frustration and exhaustion we witness in our world.

Second, once we do bank the ten million, get the beach house, or the Porsche we've been dreaming about, we'll soon discover that these external accumulations rarely deliver the fulfillment, the happiness, or the peace of mind we hoped to experience in the first place. Research shows that after weeks, maybe a few months, of elation the daily grind kicks in and our emotional thermometer falls back to our preprogrammed state – after all is done, we end up feeling how we usually felt.

When I packed my bags and moved to California, for example, I had a healthy bank account, quit my job in the old world, and set up a new life in sunny Santa Barbara. With a financial buffer, a beautiful place overlooking the Pacific Ocean and the Santa Barbara Channel Islands, and complete freedom to do whatever tickled me, it felt like heaven. But only a few months later, my all-too-familiar feeling states started returning. A sense of pressure from the workload I had recreated for myself and the same nagging feeling from my previous life in Munich: something was missing. The Essences of independence, peace of mind, and general happiness that I had felt upon my arrival became more and more overshadowed as my familiar state of being spread throughout my days.

The third reason why creating an Essence-rich experience is such a powerful consciousness shift is that we're able to experience the Essences we desire in life right here and now. While the house on the beach could be decades away, or completely beyond our reach, we can create the exact same Essences that we associate with the house in many other ways. Let's assume one Essence you seek when you imagine sitting in your beach home overlooking the wide blue ocean is the feeling of freedom. You're able to create the same feeling of freedom with other experiences: a walk on the beach, riding your bike, or jogging in the forest. Our brain doesn't differentiate how we experience an emotion. Whether it's your beach house or a walk through the woods that's giving you the feeling of freedom, the same regions in your brain fire up. Either way, your life experience blossoms.

Lastly, the more we're able to create an Essence-rich life, the more we "become" the Essence we're looking to experience. It's physics – the principle of resonance. Let's assume that you've set a material goal: financial freedom. You want the ten million in your account. With stage two consciousness, you expect that wealth will grant you the success and financial freedom you've been working for, but as you examine the deeper drivers of your goal, you discover what you're really looking for is more freedom and peace of mind. As you move to stage three energy, you start focusing on creating more of those feeling states in your life. You take walks, you meditate, you take things a little easier, and eventually arrive at the conclusion that, no matter what, you'll be fine.

Each time you schedule your walk and sit down to meditate, you experience the freedom and peace of mind you've been seeking. Each time you expand those feeling states, you "become" more of them. From your deeper state of being, you radiate more freedom and peace of mind into the world. As you do, you notice that other people start to gravitate toward you, other possibilities that provide more freedom and peace show up for you. New opportunities to expand your feeling of freedom and peace of mind appear in your life. You're living in stage three. Life isn't happening *by* you anymore. Life's happening *through* you, without the need to reach a particular destination, get places, or accumulate more external things to make you happy.

Along the way, you realize that life's a feeling experience, not a doing or having experience. We can own all the riches of the world, but if our Essences remain unfulfilled – when we don't feel the sense of freedom, joy, ease, or abundance that drives us – life sucks. When our Essences get fulfilled, life blossoms.

Why You Do Everything

As you discover the Essences that drive you, you'll be surprised to find yourself seeking to fulfill many of the same Essences in every area of your life, from money and career to family relationships, personal development, and health. If you seek more freedom in your career, it's likely that you also appreciate a sense of freedom in your relationships; and a scheduled vacation where you follow a tour guide from tourist site to tourist site probably isn't your cup of tea either. If you want more money because it gives you peace of mind, it's likely that you also want peace of mind in your health or career.

Your entire life, whether you're thirty or fifty, whether you're rethinking your career or looking to improve a relationship, is driven by ten to fifteen Essences. That's it. This bouquet of your Essences motivates and energizes you. When they get fulfilled, you rise with zest in the morning. When they remain unfulfilled – no matter whether your bank account is empty or full – you'll drag your feet and feel dissatisfied, frustrated, or resentful about your life circumstances.

If you ask me, knowing these deeper drivers sounds more fulfilling than strategizing about my career, thinking how to improve my relationship, reflecting on how to have more fulfillment and purpose in my life, or the countless other little things we wonder how to change or improve, hoping that they'll make us happier. Wouldn't it be much easier to go directly to the source: to understand which Essences are missing and how to best strengthen them?

When I shared these same ideas about Essences with Tom, my investment banker client from Connecticut, he quickly realized his dilemma and what to do about it. The positions and companies he shortlisted for his next job fulfilled his Essences for appreciation and financial abundance, but they didn't fulfill his Essences for fulfillment and connection. He saw that if he didn't find a job that would fulfill all of these Essences, he'd continue feeling frustrated and unfulfilled. His eyebrows raised further when I asked him which Essences his upscale lifestyle fulfilled. "Significance and appreciation," he responded. After a pause he added, "But I really want more joy, freedom, and deeper connections in my life. I don't think the way we currently live is the right setup to provide that."

We discussed in our following sessions how he could shift things in his personal environment. We also assessed firms and positions in the finance world that would allow him to fulfill his Essences for appreciation and abundance *and* his Essences for fulfillment and connection. It wasn't easy for Tom to make these adjustments. It had taken years to set up his lifestyle, and to let some of those aspects go in favor of fulfilling all four Essences and possibly reentering the workforce at a lower salary took courage and multiple conversations with his wife. However, these conversations in themselves created a deeper connection and intimacy in their relationship. He knew that these steps were necessary if he wanted to live an authentic life – a life in which he was courageously making choices based on Essence instead of future outcome. Life started happening through him.

Bringing Essences into Your World

Making decisions based on Essence rather than expected outcome is a simple yet extremely powerful shift to improve your life and overall sense of well-being. Simple, but not easy in a world that's driven by material goals and outcomes. When your boss tells you to increase sales by twenty percent, it's not the wisest response to let him know that his demand doesn't fulfill your Essence for ease and joy. But looking at the situation from a different perspective makes it clear that focusing only on the outside goals – demanding a twenty percent sales increase without even considering the Essences that drive the employees who are working to deliver upon the boss's request – is exactly the reason why we're burned out, why our world isn't sustainable, and why we haven't gotten a handle on the rampant levels of disengagement in our workforce.

We'll focus on how to bring Essences into our work world in Chapter 9, and why Essences have broad effects on leadership, team performance, and organizational culture. Essences are the deep drivers that motivate every person inside an organization. They bring the values of a team to life, they're critical for healthy decision-making, and they're the key for building an engaged workforce. Just imagine the engagement and energy of an organizational culture where people's Essences get fulfilled. But more about that later.

For now, let's focus on your personal Essences and how you can use them for your own benefit in all areas of your life. For that purpose, I encourage you to complete the exercise outlined at the end of this chapter before you read on.

For the exercise, select your own bouquet of twelve to fifteen Essences that drive all areas of your life. You might find a few more or a few less, but most people's lives are steered by about a dozen Essences – such as joy, creativity, ease, connection, or freedom – no matter whether they're looking at their profession, their personal relationships, or the vacations they enjoy. You'll find a list of Essences in the exercise.

Second, look through your selection of Essences and determine which ones are getting fulfilled and which ones you'd like to strengthen. You might get the Essence of creativity fulfilled in your work but still seek to strengthen fulfillment, joy, or connection.

Third, come up with experiences and events that help you fulfill the Essences you want to strengthen. Find things you can put into your calendar: a weekly yoga session or morning meditation to enhance connection, or time to get together with a friend once a week to strengthen joy.

Lastly, when you interact with others – your spouse, your children, family members, your team members or boss – try to understand their Essences. Ask yourself how you could be of service to them in fulfilling their Essences. I promise you that you'll create happy people around you. Just one recommendation: be careful of serving unhealthy relationships in this way or your tank can quickly run empty.

When we make choices based on Essence, we're authentic. We tap into a source of energy and strength that has previously remained hidden from us. Even in situations of worry or fear when the Model of Dominance & Subservience with its scarcity mindset dominates our thinking, we can use Essences to find a pathway out of the dilemma. There's always an abundance of Essence available to us. When we're short on money, yet we know that what we're actually missing is a sense of freedom or abundance, there are many ways we can nurture that feeling, even in the most dire situation. Even prisoners who experience an obvious scarcity of freedom were able to discover a sense of freedom after working on their Essences, despite still being locked up behind bars. In the words of William Ernest Henley, who inspired Nelson Mandela during his incarceration on Robben Island, "It matters not how strait the gate, how charged with punishments the scroll, I am the master of my fate, I am the captain of my soul."

The previous chapters have laid out the BE – DO – HAVE success model – the possibility to show up being who you're here to *be*, to *do* what your unique gifts and talents inspire, and to create a life in which you *have* fulfillment of your Essences. As you show up in the world that way, you're present, strong, and centered in who you are, ever expanding your overall well-being and happiness.

At this point, many wonder whether living by the new success model allows for enough direction or goal orientation. After all, having clear goals has the power to align people and release an enormous amount of energy. How can we consolidate living by the new success model and still get things done? If we still want to access that same energy source that's released by having common goals – yet without constantly striving to reach a destination and falling back into the old success model of doing more and accumulating results – we need to access another source of power and direction, one that can coexist with the new success model.

The power of purpose.

Reflection: Discover Your Essences

Discover your bouquet of Essences in the exercise, which is accessible for free in the Plan BE Online Course (https://learn. plan-be.us). Access the course at the link or QR code below and download the free available exercise in the section titled "Your Deepest Drivers: Why You Do Everything."

CHAPTER 7

Your Life Purpose and Your Soul Purpose

"A man without a purpose is like a ship without a rudder – never likely to reach home port."

– Thomas Carlyle

In 2017, an email showed up in my inbox: "Peter, I really need to find out what I want to do with my life." It was Ann, the Fortune 100 manager from Chapter 1. She had participated in one of our leadership programs, and, being a senior manager with a stellar career, she had the life many of us strive for: a happy marriage, beautiful family, cushy house, and good health. And yet, something was missing. She was missing purpose.

When I interacted with her in our program, I could see that she lived her authentic personality and was able to express her unique gifts and talents in her position. She was even aware of the Essence approach and her own bouquet of Essences, which included freedom, contribution, ease, accomplishment, and joy. Essentially, she was one of the lucky ones who already lived by the BE – DO – HAVE success model, to some extent. And yet, she felt that unreachable itch that something was still missing. She was successful, but to what end? *What was the purpose of it all*, she asked herself. Like many of us, she had arrived at a point of insight in her life where she realized that there was a higher order to reach. Something which would fill that hard-to-describe void we sometimes feel. Somehow she knew that once she was able to find that, she'd leave our three-dimensional go-go world behind and access a glimpse of who she was really here to be, her soul's purpose.

The search for meaning has been the steadfast companion for humans for thousands of years. Now that human existence has risen above mere survival, this search is moving into focus for more and more people. It can even throw people into an existential crisis; a crisis that doesn't make the media and yet it is a pervasive and growing one, demonstrated by the increasing use of antidepressants and narcotics. Maybe our search for purpose is becoming one of the strongest indicators that our model of success is simply not working anymore.

I felt the same itch for years in my own career. Always present, but hidden behind a veil, just beyond my reach. I had tried to lift the veil in various ways: I booked Ayurveda retreats in Sri Lanka, changed jobs, bought new cars, remodeled the kitchen, and engaged in sexual relationships, hoping that these would provide answers or at least fill my inner void for a few months. I created experiences that fulfilled my Essences of joy, freedom, and connection. Skiing in the Alps was one of my go-to remedies. Another one was booking vacations to beautiful places. But the respite these escapes granted from my search for meaning grew shorter and shorter.

It all culminated one overcast winter day when I decided to get another fix on the slopes of Kitzbühel in Austria. I stood on the top of the mountain, a run of perfect moguls in front of me. But the smile on my face was gone. Just chasing my Essences for joy or freedom couldn't fill the void anymore. My soul was calling. There's a substitute for making money, for exercising, even for sex – but there's no substitute for purpose.

The Power of Purpose

Author Gary Zukav created wonderful imagery about purpose in one of his books: "We're little boats on a vast ocean – paddling to the right, to the left, catching a good wind, but ultimately wondering whether there's a mothership we belong to." Your purpose is the mothership, and your inner search is the yearning to align your work and life with the mothership. You know you've come to that crossroads when you're successful at work and yet you find yourself wondering about the point of it all; when you look around and see all the things that aren't working anymore. At some point you start wondering about the bigger, more meaningful impact you're here to make in the world. As David Brooks describes: "When you've successfully climbed the first mountain in your life, created a good career, some wealth, maybe a family, realizing that it's a mountain that doesn't provide you with the well-being and satisfaction you've been looking for – wondering what your second mountain in your life will be."

Purpose provides an answer to these questions, and, despite its importance for living a fulfilled life, few people are clear about their purpose. And after our purpose is revealed to us, we discover that it's an even greater challenge to create a life that becomes an expression of our purpose. We live in a world where purpose has become more paramount than ever: more than 80 percent of Generation Y is born with a personality that wants to work and live with purpose. This is not a fashion trend. It's an evolutionary development that started in the sixties, with purpose-driven leaders like Mahatma Gandhi, Nelson Mandela, J.F. Kennedy, Martin Luther King Jr., and Mother Teresa making headlines

– in many cases losing their freedom or their life for taking a stand for their purpose. The urge to live a purpose-driven life is an evolutionary development, which will only grow stronger in the decades to come.

Consequently, being purpose-driven rather than goal-driven is becoming more important for organizations as well. Younger generations make up more of our workforce, and a growing number of customers resist supporting companies that don't make a positive impact. While the mental construct of setting goals and venturing out to achieve them – without even asking why – was the go-to business model so far, the emotional construct of purpose will be the model for the future. This is a transformative approach to business because goals are an ego-centric approach focused on accumulation while purpose is a world-centric approach focused on contribution. In the words of former Starbucks CEO Howard Schultz, "When you're surrounded by people who share a passionate commitment around a common purpose, anything is possible."

An increasing number of stories show that purpose isn't just another trend. After Paul Polman, one of our faculty members in the Conscious Business Master Program, took over the helm of consumer goods giant Unilever, he turned his entire conglomerate toward a common purpose: to improve the life and well-being of people. A straightforward doctrine, yet incredibly powerful considering that simple hygiene with Unilever's soaps could save millions of lives every year and allow millions of children to survive beyond the fifth year of their life. Under Polman's courageous leadership, Unilever outperformed its competitors and thrived as an organization – both internally and financially. It became the third most searched-for company in the world, after Google and Apple, with over two thousand people applying for job openings. A dream scenario in a world where talent is becoming an increasingly scarce resource.

But our search for purpose isn't just a personal matter. As a species, we don't have time to dabble anymore, preoccuping ourselves with our own advancement or profits. Our world is at a critical stage of evolution where we must rethink everything we do – from the way we consume products to the way we practice law or feed our children. "Our wonderful planet is 4.6 billion years old," argues Paul. "If we figuratively shrink that scale to 46 years, human beings have only been here for four hours, the industrial revolution started one minute ago, and in this minute, we've lost over 50 percent of the world's forests."

Our search for purpose has become a matter of our soul, our collective human family, and possibly our survival as a species.

Finding Your Purpose

When I was sitting in my venture capitalist office, pondering the ways to find my purpose, I made the choice to travel deep into the Amazon to work with a renowned shaman, Don Agustin Rivas. Maybe he would be able to help me find what I was looking for. In the summer of 2001, I embarked on the plane to Lima to meet up with my friend, Russell, who had recommended the journey to me. Together, we were about to spend two weeks deep in the Amazon rainforest, immersing ourselves in a series of Ayahuasca ceremonies – the sacred natural plant medicine of the Andean shamans, which had provided people with a cure for their illnesses, glimpses into other realities, or clarity for one's path for centuries.

After flying to Iquitos to gather with fellow venturers from around the world, our group – including managers seeking for a cure for their cancer and European royalty – embarked on a six-hour boat ride early the next morning to travel to the remote jungle village of Tamshiyacu, from which we trekked another few miles deep into the jungle. After our multi-day journey, arriving in Don Agustin's healing camp among the towering trees of the rainforest, surrounded by noises from birds, monkeys, and countless other creatures was like sucking Mother Earth's abundance through a straw. We lounged in the warm rainwater pools and visited with each other, carefree about what the days ahead of us would bring.

After a long night's sleep and a casual morning in the jungle, Don Agustin brought us together after lunch and asked us to perform a skin cleansing ritual in preparation for the ceremonies. Handing us a potion in a small container, he only mentioned to avoid the "sensitive" parts of our bodies with a brief comment: "Don't do it there. It'll hurt."

We smeared our naked bodies and followed his instructions with care, then continued basking in the afternoon sun. After an hour, we jumped into the pools, rubbed the potion off, and wandered off to dinner. The next morning came as a shock for many of us. We woke up blue. Literally, our skin had turned dark blue, from our hairline to our toes, sparing only the sensitive areas. As I looked into the only book-sized mirror in camp, I barely recognized myself. I had lost part of my identity overnight. Still today, I'm not sure about any benefit of the potion other than checking my known identity at the door. But with the blue skin, which lasted for nearly two weeks, one thing was sure: we couldn't bail, leave camp, and step on a plane to go home.

The Ayahuasca ceremonies took place at dusk and lasted for six to eight hours, deep into the night. As I prepared for one of the ceremonies, I set the intention to find out my purpose. I prayed, asking for help and guidance before entering the wood-built, palm-covered temple in the center of camp. As I was taking my seat on the simple bench that stretched along the inside walls of the temple, I felt anxious, wondering what the ceremony would bring, but even more anxious about the unpleasant side effects of the medicine.

Not only is its taste worse than drinking a cup of rotten milk, every seat in the temple comes equipped with a "televiseur," Don Agustin's tongue-in-cheek name for a plastic jug to purge your guts into, if needed. He added with a grin: "That's the moment when we let go and get the best visions." If that wasn't enough, I also glanced with unease at each of his helpers, four mid-fifty-year-old stout ladies who would help us go to the bathroom during the ceremony, if needed. Not out of kindness, but because the medicine tends to rob us of our bodily coordination, making us reliant on the strength of two helpers if we don't want to totter around and collapse like a marionette without a master the very moment we get up from our seat.

As the room grew dark and quiet, the medicine taking its effect and Don Agustin commencing his incredible six-hour marathon of shamanic songs, I was all but relaxed. Anticipating visions, revelations, answers – anything – I just sat in darkness, worried to let myself go and having to use the "televiseur." I hate feeling sick.

Until a few hours later, when I said to myself, *I've traveled halfway around the globe to experience this, and now I'm worried about getting sick?* The moment I let go, I started hearing voices. Not literally, more like a knowingness of what someone would say without uttering a word. "I'm not here to tell you your purpose," I sensed. Deep in trance and wide awake at the same time, I responded in silence: "Why not?" "Because if I told you your purpose, I would take away your power," I heard. Beyond the words that I perceived, it was immediately clear to me that "telling us what to do" would take away our free will and choice – one of the fundamental gifts of life. But I was left with another question: "If you're not here to tell me, how do I find out about my purpose?" "Follow what you're passionate about – what inspires you. That's how you'll find your purpose," I heard. It certainly wasn't what I wanted to hear at the time, but those words exactly described the stepping stones that helped me find my purpose several years later.

After our time in the jungle concluded, I traveled directly from Peru to the Bermudas for our investment team meeting. Still counting the remaining patches of blue on my body as I sat on the bed in my cabana at the five-star Elbow Beach Resort, I felt alien, as if I had just returned from another planet. I looked out onto the azure ocean, reflecting on my experience in the Amazon when I knew that the events in Peru weren't over yet. Behind the scenes, I felt that things were being put in motion. I felt different, realizing that I hadn't just been given words and insights about my purpose during the ceremony. Beyond words, I had received an energy of belonging and connectedness, which ultimately gave me the courage to follow my soul's calling. I knew what I needed to do.

Bringing Your Purpose into Your Life

Back in Munich, I decided I would speak to my venture capital partners about shifting the focus of my work. I'm a people person, and rather than grinding through financial models and contracts, I wanted to be out in the world, speaking about our work, and finding the top companies to invest in. I wanted to support people in finding a life they love and help build really cool companies around their purpose – that's what inspired me. To my amazement, I didn't need to lift a finger. A week after my return, two of our senior partners came into my office and asked me whether I'd be interested in taking over the coverage sector for the firm – to venture out into the world, from Rome to Paris, from San Francisco to London – and find the best companies for us to invest in.

When the student is ready, the teacher will appear. From my own path, and in helping hundreds of individuals on their path to purpose, I learned that the way we manifest our purpose in life is to start walking toward it. Once we make the decision to express our gifts and talents and follow those things that inspire us and bring us Essence, we're on track – even though we might not know what the next stepping stone will be or when it will appear in front of us. Start gently, consistently discarding those things in life that don't feed your soul. Make new choices. Take a coach. Start speaking your truth – to your spouse, to your friends, to your colleagues. Engage in opportunities that allow you to express more of what you want to create in the world. Get on stage, even if it scares your pants off. As you start walking, things will happen that you couldn't possibly have imagined or planned.

Here's just one of the many synchronicities I've experienced on my own journey: When I decided to leave the venture capital world for good, I told my mentor that I wanted to quit the firm on March 31, 2003. I was done and wanted to move back to California to pursue what I *really* wanted to do. Taking a six-week notice period into account, I planned to let my partners know about my decision by February 15. However, during conversations with my mentor, she told me that it wasn't the right time yet. Following the intuitions and messages she received, I was supposed to wait. Reluctantly, I did. The days passed, and still I was told to wait. By now it was early March, and I was certain that I had lost my window of opportunity to pack my bags in April and head out across the Atlantic.

Then, on the morning of March 8, my team and I noticed that our two senior partners didn't come to the office. Nobody in the office knew what was going on or where they were. Early in the afternoon, they walked through the door and asked our small investment team to gather in the conference room. Gloomy faced, they told us that they had just returned from an ad-hoc board meeting in Stockholm, and that our Munich office was closing due to the slow recovery of the markets after the internet bubble burst. While my colleagues sat in shock, I tried to avoid a broad smile expanding across my face. "When is this supposed to happen," I asked. "We'll keep finance people for a few weeks longer, but we'll close our offices on March 31," they responded. As I walked home from the office that afternoon, I felt a sense of elation and unbridled joy, which I had rarely felt before. It was as though I had stepped into resonance with the universe and pure energy was washing through my body, the feeling of being in the flow.

Unfortunately, the feeling of flow didn't last long. I quickly learned that once we take steps toward our purpose, doors will open, but we also face challenging times. Some people will love it when you speak about your purpose, but some family members or people in your professional life will shake their head or turn their back. The more you express your innermost thoughts, desires, convictions, and purpose, the more naked and transparent you show up in the world. The ability to hide behind a facade of a title, a company product, or a body of research disappears. You're the product, and although a title can support your standing, there's no title that can stand for your purpose. You're your own masterpiece, which some will love, and others won't. There's no need to convince anyone or to take it personally.

Your Soul's Purpose and Your Life Purpose

During the night of my Ayahuasca ceremony in the Peruvian jungle, I obtained another insight: We all have a "life purpose" as well as a "higher purpose of our soul." In order to live a happy and fulfilled life, we must balance both – an insight that could have saved Tony Hsieh's life.

Tony was a figurehead for bringing purpose into the business world. As CEO of the internet shoe retailer Zappos, he had created a company spirit and a common purpose for his company that made global headlines. Managers from around the world traveled to the Zappos headquarters in Las Vegas to learn what it takes to build a truly inspiring company culture and align every team member around a common purpose.

Zappos' purpose was to Deliver Happiness – something that customers could experience with pretty much every interaction. When Tony was invited to keynote at a conference in Chicago, his team had researched that the weather would likely turn from sun to rain on the day of his speech. At the conclusion of the conference, the rain had started. Tony positioned himself by the exit doors and handed each participant an umbrella – courtesy of Zappos. Delivering Happiness in a way that not many CEOs of billion-dollar firms would do.

Zappos customer Zaz Lamarr had ordered multiple pairs of shoes from the company, but her mum had just passed away and she just didn't have time to try the shoes on. "When I came home from the hospital this last time," Zaz shares, "I had an email from Zappos asking about the shoes . . . . so I replied that my mom had died but that I'd send the shoes as soon as I could. They emailed back that they had arranged with UPS to pick up the shoes, so I wouldn't have to take the time to do it myself. I was so touched. That's going against corporate policy. The next day, when I came home from town, a florist delivery man was just leaving. It was a beautiful arrangement in a basket with white lilies and roses and carnations. Big and lush and fragrant. I opened the card, and it was from Zappos. I burst into tears. I'm a sucker for kindness, and if that isn't one of the nicest things I've ever had happen to me, I don't know what is."

Tony ingrained the purpose to Deliver Happiness in everything Zappos did. But it wasn't only Zappos' purpose – it was also Tony's own purpose. After he left the company in 2020, he continued focusing his life laser-like on that purpose: to hack the human brain so that we can reach higher states of happiness, awareness, and creativity.

But Tony's life purpose ultimately led to his death. He was so determined to pursue his purpose that people around him found him unable to simply be present. He always had to be on the move, diving deeper into his explorations. According to reports of friends and former staff, he wasn't able to be alone or sit still. Shortly before his death, COVID demanded for people to be isolated with not much room to *do*. To circumvent this problem, he hired his friends to live with him in his mansion in Colorado. Everyone around him, even his close friends, were on his payroll.

On the morning of November 18, 2020, Tony was trapped in a house fire in New London, Connecticut. After being transported to Bridgeport Hospital to undergo treatment, he died a few days later from his burns and smoke poisoning, two weeks before his forty-seventh birthday. News reports suggested that nitrous oxide, which Tony used to explore different realities, played a role in the fire and his death.

If we want to live a healthy *and* purpose-driven life, it's crucial to balance our life purpose with our soul purpose. While each one of us has an individual life purpose, we all share the same soul purpose: to remember who we're here to be on a grander scale, to expand into our authentic power, to grow as humans and as a collective, and to graduate from this earth's classroom for overcoming our fears and limitations. Ultimately, our soul's purpose is to be fully present in the moment, with every experience that's in front of us – whether it's standing on a mountaintop in awe of the surrounding beauty or the painful experience of losing a loved one.

While our life's purpose is about Doing something on this earth, our soul's purpose is about Being. Something that Tony found challenging.

We can see our common soul purpose expressed all around us, in a blossoming cherry tree or a blooming rose. The rose's sole purpose is to be a rose. Unlike humans, it doesn't even attempt to be something it is not. It doesn't attempt to be a tulip, nor does it hold back in any way from being a rose because it feels it could do something wrong. It's not worried that others might not like it or that someone might come along and cut it. Just like for each one of us, the purpose of the flower is to be who it's here to be. Present in the moment. Fearless.

When you're able to stay present, every event, struggle, or success in your life contributes to the fulfillment of your soul's purpose. You cannot fail at this. Even if you fail in your relationships or lose your job, know that it's your way to grow in the grander scheme of things. When you're able to stay in the present moment, there's no question about purpose. Only when we disconnect from the flow of life will the itch for purpose return. When you feel frustrated because it's ten o'clock at night and you're still finalizing the presentation for your boss, the moment you become fed up quarreling with your spouse, or when you feel stressed because you only have twenty minutes to eat lunch before your next meeting – that's when the traditional model of thinking takes over. We exit the present moment, wanting things to be different than they are or we start living in a future moment.

In those moments, we revert to the realm of Doing. We disconnect from our soul's purpose and all too often ignore our soul's nudge to pay attention and realign with our higher purpose.

Aligning with Your Soul's Purpose

Two stepping stones keep us aligned with our soul's purpose: awareness and consciousness. If we want to stop the rat race or move away from doing more all the time, the first stepping stone is to become aware of our state of being. It's an ongoing practice of mindfulness to notice whether we're present and centered, or whether we're carried along on an emotional wave of frustration, stress, time-pressure, worry, or caring about the future.

These emotional states aren't bad; they're part of human existence. The distinction is whether we're aware of our emotional states, able to *be* present with these emotions, or whether they take over our thoughts and actions, catapulting us into the Model of Dominance & Subservience where we usually feel we just need to *do* what needs to get done. The doorway to remaining connected to our soul's purpose is to remain aware and mindful with what's going on inside of us – right here and now.

But even people with a high level of awareness can lead an ego-centered life and make everything about their personal advancement or gain. A spiritual teacher who uses his role to attract intimate partners would be one example. Only when we add the second stepping stone – to live with a consciousness that's interconnected to all-there-is and to be part of a bigger picture – will we be able to align with our soul's purpose. The spiritual perspective of oneness ultimately creates the necessary evolutionary shift to transform the way we work and live, and it also connects your soul's purpose with your life's purpose through a new perspective.

Truly holding the consciousness that we're interconnected makes it impossible to harm the other because we know that we're ultimately harming ourselves. It makes it impossible to create a business that's burning people out or harming the environment because we know that we're ultimately destroying ourselves. Of course, we forget. We go back to work, day in and day out, maybe even join a business that reduces carbon emissions or helps build a better company culture, but if we don't live with the awareness of this higher perspective, we'll eventually find that the impact we're trying to have remains limited.

When we forget to balance our life's purpose with our soul's purpose, we run the risk of burning out or creating detrimental experiences in our life, like Tony Hsieh and many other purpose-driven individuals who are exhausted from making a difference in the world, yearning for a respite.

As I conclude this section, you'll get the opportunity to discover your individual purpose. With that paradigm in your bag of goodies, you'll have the model and the pathway for bringing the BE – DO – HAVE success model to life and transforming the way you live and work. You know now that everything changes when you *Be* authentically yourself, *Do* what your gifts inspire, and create a life that's filled with Essence – all supporting the direction of your purpose.

In the next section, you'll understand how to take your authentic self into a world that's mostly driven by the existing DO – ACCUMULATE – BECOME success paradigm, and how to create deep and meaningful connections as a foundation for your overall happiness and success. I'll explain how to bring your authentic personality into the work world as you maneuver the road bumps along the way and how to create more inspiring organizations – companies that embrace the shift from a focus on money and profits to creating places where people can be themselves, feel belonging, and create outstanding things together.

Reflection: Discover Your Purpose

The simple and free exercise in the Plan BE Online Course (https://learn.plan-be.us) has helped countless professionals find their purpose, and I hope it will help you clarify yours. Use the link or below QR code to access the course and you'll be able to download the exercises in the Purpose section.

PART 2

Bringing the New Success Model Into the World

CHAPTER 8

Healthy Relationships: Plan BE at Home

"Your overall success in life is directly related
to the quality of your relationships."
– Me

In 1938, Harvard researchers initiated what has now become the longest-running study on happiness in the world. For more than 80 years, the Harvard Study of Adult Development has followed 724 participants from various economic and social backgrounds to find out what makes a happy life. Over the years, the researchers gathered a pile of health information, and every two years they interviewed participants about their emotional and mental well-being. They discovered a close correlation between our happiness and the quality of our relationships. According to the research, even our health and success in life is directly related to the quality of our relationships.

Of course, you could point to people who have reached success with dysfunctional or even destructive relationships, some corporate CEOs and even presidents of nations jump to mind. But where these individuals experience a breakdown in their relationships, their happiness and overall success declines; for example, when a CEO comes home from work and runs their family just like their business, expecting their partner and children to perform like their employees. In the political arena, it's even harder to imagine a happy life amidst an armada of conflicts, finger-pointing, and political maneuvering. Ultimately, we all learn this from firsthand experience: the moment one of our important relationships suffers, our happiness, well-being, peace of mind, and overall success take a dip too.

Every issue people bring into our coaching sessions or programs – from dissatisfaction with their job to seeking clarity for a business decision – has a relationship component. Even fear of rejection, grappling with a physical ailment, or worrying about money ultimately mirrors a relationship breakdown – maybe to ourselves, our values, or to our self-worth.

Life's a multiplayer game. If we want to create anything, it ultimately requires relating with others. This chapter moves from the "Me" to the "We," helping you live authentically while building deep, fulfilling relationships, and gracefully maneuvering those relationships that have become challenging or sour.

Managing the Road Bumps

When you change your life's path, especially as profound as expanding into your authentic power, things will shift in your life. With your consciousness expanding, the frequency of how you operate and show up rises. For example, you might start to resonate at C-sharp instead of B-flat. You'll realize that some of the activities, people, and events you might have previously enjoyed simply don't resonate for you anymore. They're at B-flat while you're now at C-sharp. The dissonance hurts, and it can become more difficult for you to join the bar nights you used to go to, eat the food you used to eat, mingle in the big cities you used to enjoy, or spend time with the people you used to hang out with, family members included. You might not know exactly why certain activities or relationships aren't working anymore. You might even wonder what's wrong with you when the interactions that seemed so normal for years suddenly drain your energy.

You're growing a new self, a new identity, which at the beginning of your journey to authentic success is still a tender seedling, only able to blossom in a nurturing environment. When we decide to close the gap between our conditioned and authentic personality, we're uprooting ourselves from our old identity, beliefs, and security mechanisms and transplanting ourselves into a new world. Our roots need time to regrow, and any criticism or judgment makes our newfound life vulnerable. At the same time, in order to grow strong in our authentic power, we need some headwind – just like plants that are grown inside a greenhouse need artificial wind to grow strong and survive after they're planted outside the greenhouse.

Expanding into your authenticity is like traveling to a foreign land. You're not familiar with how things work or if they will work out in the way you hope. Unfamiliar with the rules of the new land, it's easy for you to second-guess your choices. Frankly, when you follow your authentic path, start speaking your truth, or even change professions, you might not know whether things will work out at all. When I left the venture capital world and moved to California, I didn't know whether I was actually going to find a better way to work or just wasting the most productive years of my life. For years, I felt the pressure of this uncertainty as I watched my former colleagues and friends grow in their careers and even retire before I got started.

The biggest challenge on our path to authenticity is the fear of uncertainty. As a result, many people stay put in their familiar environment for decades, hoping for circumstances to change. Our mind reminds us that if we stay in our job, at least we have *some* certainty about what our current way of life will provide for us: a steady paycheck, steady relationships – both healthy and unhealthy – and a job title that has become part of our identity.

As I'm writing these lines, I'm riding on the train down the California coast. Slow as it goes. In the row behind me, a forty-something-year-old woman just shared with her three girlfriends in a shaking voice: "Every Sunday I get these dark moments because I hate the company that I need to go back to every Monday morning." How serendipitous.

How long do we stay in our work routines because they provide us with certainty – and in her case, the funds to spend $1,200 on a dinner during a lush weekend trip to Santa Barbara with her girlfriends – but little space for us to expand into who we're truly here to be?

On your path to authentic power, your fear of uncertainty will be a steadfast companion that you'll want to make friends with. When it surfaces, know that it's here to build your identity and inner strength to remain centered and empowered during challenging and uncertain situations and to help you stand in the fire and grow the character and *chutzpah* to be the leader others will trust.

The quality of your life ultimately depends on your relationships: to yourself, to others, to nature, and to material things like money. The following principles, guidelines, and experiences will help you apply the new success model to your relationships so that in your connections with others you can *Be* authentically yourself, *Do* what inspires you together, and *Have* the Essences such as flow, well-being, connection, love, and inspiration, which you and your relations seek to create.

Relating to Yourself

Building healthy relationships with others starts with building a healthy relationship with yourself. If you find it hard to love yourself because you carry extra weight or you're lying awake at night worrying about your job, it's only a matter of time until your frustration, worry, or self-criticism seeps into your relationships. This self-criticism creates a veil through which you relate to the people around you. Perhaps you're thinking of your extra weight when your partner embraces you; or your mind replays your worries when you ask your boss for a pay raise. Either way, if the relationship to ourselves is disturbed, it's hard to be present with the person across from us. It's as though our being is clouded.

Of course, we don't enjoy the negative feelings about our weight and our worries. So, to improve the situation, we usually employ the old success model: we *do* something, expecting that we'll *become* happier with ourselves. We schedule an exercise routine, start a diet, or begin any number of activities or self-improvement courses that could enhance our physical appearance and overall well-being, hoping that maybe a fancy nail design or dying the hair in our nose will do the trick and make us feel better. Nothing wrong with fancy fingernails and well-manicured nose hair, but if we expect to become happy or create deeper connections with ourselves and others in that way, we're betting on the wrong horse.

Principle 1: We can only love another as deeply as we love ourselves

To create deep and fulfilling relationships, we must first fall in love with ourselves. Not in a narcissistic or ego-centric way, but in a way where we choose love over fear or self-criticism. It's impossible to genuinely fall in love with ourselves by *doing* something more, less, or different – by earning another degree, making a bunch of money, or dieting. External achievements and activities may satisfy our ego and calm the voices in our head, but they aren't able to fill the void that lies beneath our self-criticism or comfort us when we don't feel valuable, safe, or confident in our own skin. Falling in love with yourself isn't something you *do*. It's a state of Being, independent of your life's circumstances.

To reach that state of Being, remember who you're here to Be: a light being having a physical experience – not a physical being seeking a light experience. When you let this realization take space in your conscious-ness, when you remember that you're here to express your unique talent, authentic personality, and higher purpose, you'll notice an expanded state of Being in which you don't need to be anything or anyone different than who you are. Without doing a single thing, you can experience peace of mind and love for the unique individual you're here to be. Can you sense that? Suddenly, your nails, the hairs in your nose, even the extra weight become meaningless. You're at peace with where you are. You may not love your extra weight, of course, but you're able to accept it for right now. In that space of self-acceptance and love, you can be present with yourself and the people around you. No agenda; no veil. You can still work out and watch your diet, but you don't do it to fix something or to be happy. You simply do it because you care. From a place of love and inspiration instead of fear and judgment.

The same is true for all the other stories we tell ourselves about our lack of confidence, not being good enough, our self-doubt. We don't need to *get to some place* in order to love ourselves. No degree can fill up our low self-confidence; no amount of work or money will eradicate the void of not feeling good enough.

When we experience negative feelings about ourselves, we can use them for what they're here to do: to remind us that we've forgotten who we really are. We can use them as guideposts pointing us toward our wholeness. If we allow it, we can follow these signs to explore our unique gifts, be kind to ourselves, and refocus on those activities that inspire us.

Principle 2: You have to be alone to be all-one

In the spring of 2002, I bought a BMW motorcycle from my friend in Northern California. I had just quit my investment position and decided to take two months off, travel through California, and meet with people and companies that operated in a more inspiring and authentic way. I had scheduled a meeting with one of Patagonia's executives at their Ventura headquarters. To get there, my friend had recommended taking the backroads from Santa Cruz to Ventura. After a breathtaking ride though the California countryside, I checked into a simple motel in Taft, a small oil drilling town located in the middle of a barren desert landscape. When I woke up the next morning, the excitement of my motorcycle adventure had vanished. After the initial high, it dawned on me that I had left my job to search for something nebulous. I had only a hunch that there must be something out there that could provide me with a deeper sense of belonging and purpose. When I pulled back the curtains, the soulless backyard of the motel and desolate desertscape added extra weight to my mood. It dawned on me that I was journeying on my own. Although I was still married at the time and was just taking a vacation, I felt utterly alone. *Thank God*, I told myself, *I have a session scheduled with my mentor.*

When I told him about my situation, he just said: "Peter, we have to be alone to be all-one." I sat on the bed in my motel room, his words sinking in. As he continued speaking, it became clear to me that the path from our conditioned self to our authentic self is one that we ultimately walk alone. There's no cushioning, no one who goes through the exact same fears you or I experience along the way.

Being alone with our worries, demons, and fears is a natural growth process, so natural that most of the first nation peoples have institutionalized it in the form of vision quests and walkabouts. Others can accompany us to the edge of the bridge, but ultimately we must cross the bridge to living our authentic life ourselves. That quest gives us the authority and strength to lead the way for others once we reach the other side of the bridge.

When you feel alone on your path, misunderstood by friends or parents, or uncertain about your future, know that it is an important and necessary stepping stone toward your authentic power and deepening the relationship with yourself. When you're left with nothing or nobody, you're building your own identity from that nothingness. It's not an identity that's intertwined with the conditioning the world places on you; it's your authentic identity. With this new identity, you're not becoming an accountant, marketing professional, or singer because that's what your parents led you toward, but because it becomes an expression of your soul.

During these times when you feel alone, it's still helpful to build your tribe of people. Buckminster Fuller says, "Environment is stronger than willpower." Even when we have the willpower to change the way we work and live, we need an environment that allows us to grow new roots. Even if it's just one single person, like my mentor, who understands your path and situation and provides you with guidance and support. Other options are programs that support your new worldview and books or movies that help strengthen the new neural pathways you're building.

Once you cross the bridge and expand your authentic power, you enter a different world. People, activities, or interests might shift or they might stay. You won't know. What you can trust is that you'll build new connections, meet people who appreciate you for who you are, who are keen to cocreate new endeavors with you as they recognize your inherent power and resonate with your vision of what the world could look like. At that point, you just have one job left: to be abundantly yourself.

Relating to Others

On your journey to authentic power, relationships will change. You'll develop new ones that provide more depth and connection. Others will fall by the wayside or create discomfort. Your parents might worry that you've gone over the deep end; your spouse may express concern that you'll distance yourself; coworkers might get frustrated because you don't do your job like you always did; and even your relationship with yourself can get shaky when you doubt your choices and feel uncertain about your future.

Once you express your authentic personality, you'll leave parts of yourself and relationships from your conditioned environment behind. Some will be challenged by the new you. They'll criticize or misunderstand you; some will even try to hold you back because they're afraid that you'll leave them or that you're living a fantasy. Such was my parents' response, who were convinced that I was living a pipe dream when I quit my venture capital job and moved to California.

Even though friction or pushback from our existing environment is natural, it can make our uncertain path to authenticity even more draining as we attempt to stand our ground and remain true to ourselves. Expanding your authentic power requires clarity and strength. You'll be putting a stake in the ground that others will want to hold on to.

You'll be a leader for others, and you don't want that stake to fall over the moment a few people try to hold on to it. Picture the strength and fortitude Nelson Mandela gained through his years of adversity. Standing amidst adversity builds that level of inner strength, centeredness, and authority.

Principle 3: No more time for BS

People who operate at a high level of consciousness can rarely be found in bars or attending drinking parties. With your level of authenticity, clarity, and energy increasing, you have less time and patience for BS. Conversations about external circumstances – making money, arguing about politics, talking about other people or buying cars – simply become boring. The more you wake up, the more you're in the game to create meaningful conversations, deep connections, and a positive dent in the world. This can be particularly taxing because a large part of our world revolves around BS. The news, the ways businesses operate, and the products from Madison Avenue are feeding our conditioned personalities. Our entire consumer industry would need to change if it wasn't catering to our fears, worries, or deficiencies.

Picture your level of consciousness as a triangle with the base representing a lower consciousness energy and the tip being a high consciousness energy. When we live our lives with a lower consciousness energy, we're able to move from right to left without falling off the triangle. In real-world terms, this looks like endless bar nights, corporate lunches, and parties with a lot of conversations for the sake of making conversation. The more we expand our consciousness, the higher we rise on the triangle, the narrower our tolerance becomes. At the top, even if you move slightly to the left or right, you'll fall off the triangle. When you engage in situations that aren't aligned – when you resonate at C-sharp and engage in situations that resonate at B-flat – your energy drops. You lose your tolerance for BS.

This is a phenomenon many people experience who are creating more conscious lifestyles: "I love my new life," one workshop participant told me, "but I find it really challenging to keep doing the same things with my friends." Personally, I pulled my wife aside many times, feeling bad about wanting to leave the party early because I felt drained endlessly talking about football or other sports events.

Falling off the triangle trains you to determine what works and what doesn't, ultimately keeping you on track, guiding you to accepting and embodying your authentic power. On your way there, learning how to make healthy boundaries becomes crucial for maintaining your energy. Boundaries remind you to focus your energy on things that give you inspiration and joy – to play, to create meaningful conversations, and to deepen your relationships with people who feed your soul. Once your roots grow stronger and you're grounded in your authenticity, you'll be able to engage with everything and everyone; but just like me in an endless football conversation, you might choose otherwise.

Principle 4: Don't try changing others

My wife and I spent our honeymoon in Vieques, a small island just east of Puerto Rico. We had booked a boutique hotel with cabanas overlooking the Caribbean Sea. One night, I woke up at three in the morning. After laying still and listening to the ocean for a while, I decided to walk out onto the lawn that stretched between our cabana and the sea. When I looked at the stars, feeling the warm Caribbean breeze on my skin, I experienced a moment of bliss.

Everything stopped, and for no particular reason I felt elated, deeply connected to myself and everything around me, and tremendously grateful for my life and the loving relationship with my wife. "I want to be *here*, with *you*, right *now*," appeared in my mind. That was the reason for my happiness, I realized. I didn't want to be anywhere else but right there on that patch of lawn – with myself, my wife sleeping in the cabana, connected with Mother Earth. Eckhart Tolle says it in simpler terms: all stress is caused by being "here" and wanting to be "there." In that moment, I didn't have any desire to be "there." Being fully present brought a feeling of complete bliss.

When you change your life's path, you can bet that some people prefer you to be "there" – to be different. Most likely, even you want others to be "there" – to behave differently toward you, accept you for who you are, or at least understand you. When Christine, a woman in her late forties, decided to quit her manager position to pursue a more purposeful career, she found it hardest to visit her parents. "They just don't understand how I could quit my job," she told me. "They constantly worry that my choice will screw up my life and just want me to continue what I always did. They just want me to play it safe, but I can't do it anymore."

After I quit my finance position to discover a better way to work and live, I wanted my father to understand me. He, meanwhile, wanted me to stay put in my job. Of course, we both felt we were "right," but neither of us could be "right here, right now, with you." We were "here" and wanted to be "there" or wanted the other person to be "there," causing us both stress and a break down in our relationship.

We've all experienced similar situations. We want people around us – our parents, friends, or manager – to understand and support our ideas or choices. Instead, when their skepticism, criticism, or worry hits us like an orchestra playing out of tune, it drains our energy and confidence and we want to get up and leave. When we're being asked about our uncommon choices and viewpoints on our path to authenticity, our knee-jerk response is to explain ourselves and try to convince the other person so that we can get the support and love we want. But we're wasting our time. Even though we wish that others would understand us, deep down we know that some people simply aren't able to support us on our new path.

When you're in a situation where you don't get the understanding or support you want, it helps to remember that the person across from you is usually projecting their fear onto you. When my dad wasn't able to give me the emotional support I hoped for, he feared that I wouldn't make it in the world and that my chosen path would lead to disaster. Of course, his fear perfectly resonated with my own uncertainty about the future, putting us both off-kilter. In our encounters, both of us showed up with this unspoken fear – a challenging foundation for a life-giving relationship.

When you're in a relationship or situation in which you feel adversity, there's another option besides trying to change the other person or turning your back. That option is to be present with their emotions. If possible, just for a moment, forget yourself and your own story, and stay present with the fear, worry, or concern behind their words. You can even say to yourself, "Thank you for sharing your concerns with me. I see that the choices I'm making are really hard for you to understand." This provides a space for compassion and empathy where we're able to witness the pain and struggle of the other person.

Principle 5: Love where people are at

In the summer of 2022, I was invited to participate in a conference in Austin, Texas, that brought together 200 leading system's thinkers, game theorists, evolutionary biologists, business, and finance people mixed with authors in the consciousness and personal development space. Our aim was to put our heads and hearts together to cocreate a healthier and more sustainable pathway into the future for business, finance, and our world at large.

Within a few hours, we agreed our world was at an inflection point and we must develop paradigm-shifting ways to work and live if we want to sustain human life on this planet. With a common vision in place, we gathered in circles that focused around specific topics: the future of finance, sustainable living, business transformation, and so on. The topics were spot-on. The people were incredible. And yet in every circle we quickly hit a wall, with no solution in sight. In the absence of hope, we looked at each other and agreed: "Let's pop the cork and party!"

We argued with each other about what should be done, why many of the current approaches were flawed, and what must change. The more we argued, the more personal biases, thoughts, experiences, and sometimes traumas surfaced in the conversation – the need for new laws that would regulate financial markets, the need to reach racial equality before we can truly change the business system, and so on. While some argued for the best path forward, others disengaged and got frustrated by the back-and-forth. A group dynamic that's familiar to all of us.

When I sat back and observed the conversations, I noticed that in order to transform the way we work and live, we must love where people are at first. Imagine a conflicting relationship of your own; instead of wanting the person across from you to understand you or support your point of view, what if you actually love where the other person is at – truly *love* the place they're at in their lives. During an argument with your spouse, can you pause for a moment and acknowledge where they're at, without needing things to be different or wanting to get to resolution or harmony? Could you see their opinion, their resistance, their level of consciousness, their struggle in wanting to be right or understood as a flower in the bouquet of human existence? If you resisted where they're at, you'd dominate their life experience and squish their possibility for growth. When you truly love where the other is at, you'll be able to see the richness of life – the diversity of thoughts, opinions, and experiences. With this mindset conflict can become more engaging than your favorite TV show.

Taking it a step further, what if you dropped your own agenda and supported them in where they want to go? If your spouse wants to spend more time at work, can you accept that this is where his "river is flowing" and support him? If your manager wants you to increase your sales quota, can you accept where she's at and support her in her wanting to succeed? If your sister wants you to get off her back, can you accept and support her need for independence?

Ultimately, all people want is to be seen and heard. Once you enter conversations from that perspective, without the need to change people around you, resistance and conflicts start to dissolve and a common ground opens. If you also offer your support to reach their desires, without ego, you'll find the spirit and love flowing into that relationship.

This doesn't mean that you need to follow them on their journey. You're not becoming a doormat, supporting everyone else's wishes and desires but your own. "My wife told me that she wants to have sex with another man," Ken challenged this idea during a leadership program. "There's no way I can or want to support that." What if Ken could first accept that this is something his wife wants – without resisting or judging her need – and from that place of acceptance ask what she has been missing in their relationship and why she wishes for other relationships? We encouraged Ken to do so after the workshop. When he returned to the next session and shared about his conversation, he found out that she was ultimately seeking connection because he was working in another city and was only home for the weekend: "I didn't expect it, but this conversation actually brought us closer together. And I can definitely support her in creating more connections in her life. I actually *want* to do that."

Not every situation turns out that way. In a parallel scenario, his spouse might have sought out other sexual experiences anyway. If the choices of the other don't nourish our soul and we can't travel with them anymore, we can bow out of the relationship at any time. But even when we choose to do so, we can accept where the other person is headed and support them in fulfilling their deeper needs.

The more I was able to see the worries of my father, including the circumstances that led to them, I was able to understand his need for safety and fitting in. Even though I didn't get my need for understanding and support met by him until he was at an older age, our relationship became more tender and connected. All that was needed to change our relationship was to shift my focus from fulfilling my own needs to falling in love with where he was at.

If you're willing to take the principles in this chapter for a test drive, you'll find that they help create deeper connection and understanding in any relationship. Moving into the business arena, where so much of our focus is on getting things done, some of these approaches can seem unrealistic. As we continue expanding our circle from the "Me" to the "We" to the "It," in the next chapter we'll explore how to show up with our authentic power at work and how to make it possible to bring the new success model into your career and your organization.

CHAPTER 9

Creating Fulfilling Workplaces: Plan BE at Work

"I have failed for many years to empower my feminine side. Our world is suffering from hypermasculinity. We turned it into a world of doing. Go out there and do stuff! Mostly stuff that doesn't nourish anyone."
– Mo Gawdat, Former Chief Business Officer, Google X

It has become painfully obvious that traditional business approaches aren't working anymore. Despite all the perks – from ping-pong tables to free massages – more than 80 percent of professionals around the world are disengaged. Increasing numbers of employees are burning out or quitting their jobs. It has become one of the most pervasive challenges of our time to bridge our inner spiritual desires with the demands of the external world – to create a workplace where we can show up being our authentic self, to make the impact we're here to make, to create amazing things together, *and* to receive a paycheck healthy enough to sustain our family. But how is this possible in a work world that is addicted to Doing?

During a yoga retreat, meditation, or a long vacation, we might get a taste of who we're here to be – how life's supposed to be – but when we return to the office on Monday morning, our expansive sense of Being quickly vanishes as we get caught up in the clockwork office routine. Back at our desk, we're left yearning for the moments of bliss on our beach towel or yoga mat.

Like so many, we're stuck between a rock and a hard place. We don't want to give up the career, reputation, and security that has taken us years to build. But most of us also don't want to quit the work world altogether to spend our remaining days singing chants on a mountaintop. Without knowing what to do, most of us stay where we are – maybe changing jobs along the way but never quite finding out how to bring our full Beingness into the workplace, never quite able to create wholesome and authentic success.

Alex, a serial entrepreneur and owner of four businesses, was stuck in the same situation until he created a unique way for himself to bridge Being with Doing in his work. In his house in the upscale California beach town of Montecito, he dedicated one room as his inspiration office. He furnished the light-filled room overlooking the ocean with only a leather chair and a whiteboard. Every workday, Alex retreats into his inspiration office at nine o'clock and stays there until lunch time. During those three to four hours he does… nothing. He sits in the comfortable leather chair, looking out at the ocean. He just sits… and sits. He remains present. Then an idea or inspiration bubbles to the surface of his awareness. Sometimes only one idea a day. Sometimes a few more. If it's a good one, he gets up and notes it on the whiteboard, then sits back down and goes back to being present, looking at the ocean. "Since I do this morning routine, I've become incredibly effective," Alex says with a big smile. "The ideas I get are so focused – they come from such a deep place of being that I can just pick up the phone and have my team plug them into my companies."

Granted, many of us have neither the luxury nor the patience to take that amount of time to reflect. Yet, Alex offers a glimpse of how bringing our authenticity, the new success model, and a deepened sense of Being into our workplace could actually be good for business. How can we make it possible for ourselves to create the right balance of Being and Doing at work, especially if we're not at the top of the food chain with a battalion of employees executing our ideas?

The Dilemma of Our Time

I'm not going to sugarcoat the challenge of bringing the new success model into our current work world. There's no easy way to do it. I wish I could give you a quick fix to make it happen, but there is no short-cut to authenticity. Our work world is literally addicted to the existing success model. Driven by our scarcity and survival-programmed mind, it's deeply ingrained in our behavioral DNA to feel the constant need to *do* and *accumulate*. And in order to feed that perceived need, it has become commonplace for businesses and individuals to extract people's and planet's resources to fulfill our own need and fill our own pockets.

Milton Friedman made this approach the business mantra in his 1970's article in *The New York Times*, stating, "The social responsibility of business is to increase its profits." We've even gone so far as to expect people to leave behind key parts of their personality, especially the qualities of caring, empathizing, supporting, and nurturing others. These qualities are discouraged in favor of goal-orientation, linear thinking, direc-tiveness, and action-taking – qualities that are far more respected in the demanding business world. To expect that it's easy to bring our authenticity and the new success model into that kind of environment would be a setup for disappointment and frustration.

Johanna, a vice president at a global manufacturing company, was confronted with the same dilemma. She was debating staying with her current company, finding an employer where she could bring more of her authentic self to work, or setting out on her own. It was painful for her to see how people in her firm showed up every morning, working hard but leaving their heart and soul at the door. For years, she had felt a lack of purpose in her job; and even while she was getting rewards and promotions, she was quietly wondering how to create a more fulfilling way to work for herself.

Even after years of searching, she still didn't know what to do. If she were to leave her job, how would she know that her next employer would be any better? Most likely, she'd find the exact same dynamic and experience the same frustration and lack of meaning. She didn't feel comfortable venturing out on her own either. She had made it quite far up the corporate hierarchy and was worried about starting fresh. She wondered what kind of work she could do to have more fulfillment *while* maintaining her standard of success. And so, like many, Johanna remained in her job; stuck "in the meantime" rather than "on purpose," performing well to the outside, but ultimately waiting for the right time or opportunity to change her situation.

This dilemma is ubiquitous. In every country, every age group, in nearly every company. In the United States alone, Gallup research shows that more than half of all professionals are in a similar situation. But what if we're asking the wrong question altogether? What if the real dilemma isn't about changing how we work, the way our company operates, or finding a job where we can be authentic? What if the dilemma is a much bigger one: our changing evolutionary path as humans, which is playing out right in front of us, disguised as our personal dissatisfaction with the status quo. Dissatisfaction about the way we work isn't just about finding a better job or creating a happier and healthier lifestyle. It's a persistent nudge for our soul to remember who we're here to Be so that we can overcome fears that keep us small and courageously step into our authenticity.

Transforming the Way We Work: An Evolutionary Process

Our personal frustration or lack of fulfillment at work isn't just a personal problem, but a result of a global evolutionary issue. Our entire world is at a crossroads. All around the world, people are waking up and challenging every status quo: from the way we conduct business and practice medicine to the way we educate our children and eat. The existing, extractive ways of business and leadership are sucking the souls out of people and depleting our natural resources. Our personal search for a more authentic way to work and live is a mere reflection of this bigger issue. Burnout, depression, and the use of narcotics are skyrocketing. And yet, we're still pretending that everything's okay. We go to work every day and continue business as usual.

But the evolutionary pressure is rising, and millions of professionals feel the same itch for change. Eighty percent of millennials aren't interested in working for a company that doesn't make a positive social impact. Unlike previous generations, many of the younger professionals walk their talk. Generation Z adds to the pressure for businesses to change, demanding workplace cultures that can provide more genuine connection and belonging. By now, every organization is aware that they need to transform. Even though company leaders speak boldly about transformation, most are unable to change. They're addicted to the existing goal- and KPI-driven way of business. In addition, many of today's leaders have arrived in their position with the traditional way of business. It worked for them. To expect them to change in their successful roles, often at an advanced age, to try something that hasn't been widely proven yet is a setup for disappointment.

If you're lucky, you're working for an organization that follows the tides of change and encourages your authentic expression. If not, you'll likely feel like the previously mentioned stranger in a strange land. The more you expand your consciousness and show up authentically, the more you realize that you've entered into a new room of possibility that most people don't even know exists. You see the world from a different level of awareness, and as you speak from that vantage point, many people around you are simply not able to comprehend what you mean. You've upgraded your consciousness, and since there's no undo button for conscious evolution, your quest to truly live in this new realm of possibility isn't only nice to have, it becomes paramount for your well-being, happiness, and success.

The Stranger in a Strange Land

Imagine you've lived your whole life in Japan. Then you wake up one morning in Germany. You walk out onto the street and eventually figure out where you are, but people can't understand you. You walk the streets, and everything looks unfamiliar. You can't make sense of why the Germans act in certain ways, dress the way they do, eat what they eat, are a little clunkier around the edges, and don't even bow when they greet each other.

Maybe you've experienced meetings in your company where you felt the same way: people debating issues that seem strange or like a waste of time to you. Power plays, inauthentic behaviors, and dominators pushing the agenda, causing stress for everyone in the room, while others withdraw, become silent, or quietly type away on their laptops. *What am I doing here?* you ask yourself.

With your authenticity and consciousness expanding, you've literally entered a new world. You've become a stranger in a strange land. You speak with the people around you, trying to make your point from your newfound realm of consciousness in an attempt to convey to them what you see, until you realize you're essentially explaining the taste of an orange to someone who has never seen an orange before. You get blank stares, maybe some curiosity, but little genuine connection and understanding. How are you able to be yourself in that place? How is it possible to thrive in an environment where a part of you has already moved on – to truly expand into your authentic Being in a world that's mostly focused on Doing?

Being in a Doing World

As a venture capitalist, I worked until nine every night. My body was so caught up in the daily busyness of Doing – to the detriment of my marriage, my friendships, and my health – that I wasn't able to stop my mind anymore. I forced myself to take breaks after lunch and relax on a bench in the nearby park, but my mind kept spinning like a gyroscope, rattling through all the things that still needed attention. Weekend trips couldn't stop my mind from racing either. There was always more to do. *How could it be possible to Be myself – authentically and in the flow – with that level of pressure*, I wondered.

Managers tell me that they can relate. With never ending to-do lists, many yearn for a time where they can just Be. Let's face it: most of us want time to kick back, reflect, find some peace, but often even when we find some time, we fall right back into our accustomed mode of Doing – work out, throw a dinner party, fix the garden, and so on.

To "Do" more "Being" certainly can't be the right approach either. We can schedule a rigorous meditation routine, yoga classes, or retreats, even try to change outside circumstances or jobs, but when we walk back into the same system of work, we quickly fall back into our ingrained mode of Doing. To expand our sense of Being in a Doing-dominated world requires embodying our Beingness. It's about integration rather than taking action – an awareness rather than a destination. And in many cases, it involves healing those patterns, thoughts, and fears that have kept us addicted to working harder and doing more for decades.

During our Conscious Business Master Program, a manager from Argentina who had just experienced a mind-blowing psychic reading about his authentic personality asked one of our faculty members, Pamala, how he could bring that level of authenticity into his environment in a global oil and gas corporation. "I'd love to show up at work in the way you describe," he said. "But when I do that, I feel so much resistance and skepticism from my peers." Pamala responded: "When the walls in your house don't give way, go out through the roof. You need to elevate your own energy and consciousness first. We must embody our authentic power before we can bring it into the world." Then adding her own story, growing up in a religious environment as a person with psychic abilities: "When I was young, my abilities didn't just meet resistance; they were condemned. I had to fully embody my gifts and show up with an inner strength and authenticity. I moved away and worked with people from all over the world for over thirty years now. After several years, some who previously condemned me called me up and have now become long-term clients."

Ultimately, what allowed me to create more balance and stop the rat race in my mind was to focus on expanding activities that were in alignment with my authentic personality: speaking at events, looking for companies that were making a bigger impact in the world, and contributing to the well-being of leaders in my portfolio companies whenever I had the opportunity to coach them as a board member. Likewise, to balance Doing with Being in your world, take time to integrate and embody your authentic personality; and from that place of embodiment create activities and conversations that inspire you. As you do, you will notice that your Doing originates from a place of Being – from your soul. Although there's clarity and intention, there's no wanting anymore. Therefore, it will not drain you or feel like you're working.

Our journey to authentic success is not to Do something different but to become intimately familiar with our unique talent, to become clear who we're here to Be, our contribution to the world, and the value it brings to others. The deeper this clarity grows, the more you'll become confident to walk your own path, and the easier it will be to handle pushback, resistance, and adversity. You won't Do your gifts and talents anymore; you will become your gifts and talents. You won't find leaders like Nelson Mandela, Mother Teresa, or Richard Branson pushing their unique personality and talents. They've become a vessel through which their authentic expression and talents can flow.

Of course, this is easier said than done. Susan, for example, took about three years to integrate her authentic talent and show up for her clients in that way. For over twenty years, she had been working for a big computer firm, receiving awards for her leadership and moving up the ranks. But when she felt that she wasn't able to live her authenticity in the company anymore, she quit. After setting up her own marketing consulting business, she quickly became clear on what she could accomplish. She signed up global corporations as clients and helped them rethink their marketing strategy. But still she felt overworked. She hadn't embodied her authentic talents yet. She was still Doing it.

It was during a coaching conversation that her unique gift truly sank in: she realized that in everything she did she "lifted the veil" for people and gave them a sense of calm, clarity, and direction. Whenever there was uncertainty, conflict, or low performance in teams, she came in and lifted the veil. As a result, her clients became unstuck; they saw clearly what needed to be done and how to move forward. Her power was to release people's brakes.

Even then, Susan wasn't quite grasping the value of her contribution. She had done it for decades and it came so naturally to her that she wasn't able to see its true value. But once she fully integrated her gift and the value she delivered and it moved from a mental understanding of Doing to a heartfelt embodiment where she was Being the gift to the world, things changed dramatically: clients booked her for lifting the veil. And rather than needing to constantly do more to satisfy her clients – writing long proposals, discussing workshop agendas, or delivering slide decks proving the results – it became more important for her success to show up centered, present, and without her own agenda. She was Doing from a place of Being.

Ultimately, our job is to embody and fully integrate who we're here to be and to be of service to others from that place of Being. As we contribute to the world from that place, we become centered in our authenticity and grow in our inner authority. We're not Doing from a place where we need to push things forward, we're being pulled into taking action. Not because we have to, but because we want to.

From Doing to Being: Your Authentic Voice

There's no debating: if we want to create or achieve anything in life, it ultimately requires some Doing. Even though our thoughts can manifest our reality, building a product, selling a service, or bringing our purpose into the world requires more than meditating on the couch. The Bible makes an important point, "in the beginning was the word." We literally create through our words. Even the simple action of requesting a pen from another person happens through communication. Therefore, if we want to bring our authentic power into the world, developing our authentic voice is an important stepping stone.

With our authentic voice, we don't speak from a place of needing or wanting. We speak from a place of inner clarity and possibility. Watch a video of Martin Luther King Jr.'s famous "I Have a Dream" speech at the National Mall in Washington. He doesn't speak from a neediness to convince anyone. He touches and inspires the masses with a new possibility. He paints a *de facto* image of a new world. "I have a dream that my four little children will one day live in a nation where they will not be judged by the color of their skin but by their character."

John F. Kennedy speaks in the same way during his moon address at Rice University in 1962: "We shall send to the moon, 240,000 miles away, a giant rocket, more than 300 feet tall, on an untried mission to an unknown celestial body, and then return it safely to Earth."

Neither one sells their vision. They don't dwell on things that are broken. From a place of inner authority, they offer a new vision for what's possible, and those who resonate with their vision get on board. They speak with an inner clarity and independence, without the need to be accepted, validated, or patted on the back. Ultimately, we're asked to do the same to express our authenticity and purpose in the workplace. As a matter of fact, if you examine inspiring leaders in your workplace – or in other organizations, just in case your company is an inspiration desert – they speak from the same place, taking a stand despite all the differing opinions.

The more we embody and Be our authenticity and purpose, the more we'll speak our authentic voice and show up with strength and centeredness in our leadership. The more you embody your authentic power, the more it will be reflected in your words, without the need to Do anything different. People will sense the "that's-the-way-it's-going-to-be" energy beneath your words. It might sound as simple as saying, "I believe when people are truly seen for their authentic personalities, they'll access a level of clarity and power that can change our culture," versus, "We need to change our culture so that people can bring their authentic personalities." The former provides the image of a new reality; the latter expresses a "wanting."

The key to bringing your authentic power and purpose into your workplace is to speak from that place of possibility while connecting to the concrete issues or problems in your organization. For example, when there's a breakdown in trust in your team and collaboration has gone down the drain, imagine saying to your boss: "When I see breakdowns in trust and collaboration in our team, I'm concerned about our effectiveness. There's a way where we can access a completely different level of power and collaboration in our team. Can we schedule a conversation to discuss how to create that?" If you were a leader, would you make time for that conversation?

When you speak to "what's possible" versus "what's broken" you leave others touched and inspired. You open the door to solving other people's problems using your magic.

Define the Game You Play

In order to reach that level of clarity and energetic power with our words, first we must become clear about the game we choose to play. Most of today's businesses operate around goals. Determined by a few individuals at the top, the ego-based construct of goals doesn't take into consideration what people care about or what they're in the game for. Most employees across an organization donate their time and energy to fulfill the goals of individuals at the top. People roll up their sleeves and get to work, but – aside from performing well or making money – they don't even know why they do what they do. Building truly inspiring organizations requires accessing the emotional power in people. As outlined in previous chapters, we must shift from the mental construct of goals to the emotional construct of purpose: a contribution that reaches beyond ourselves or the organization. We must agree on the bigger game we play as a team – a common purpose.

To manifest the shift of an organization from a goal-driven to a purpose-driven mindset, individuals inside the organization must become aware of their own purpose first – the game *they* want to play. If we fail to accomplish that, we'll continue fulfilling other people's dreams and ambitions. Hence, an important ingredient for finding your authentic voice is to become clear about your own purpose and to speak it in a way that touches and inspires others to join your cause. That's how you show up as a leader.

When Paul Polman took over the CEO position at Unilever, he learned from former Medtronic's CEO Bill George about the importance of finding your own North Star. "When I visited company meetings at their offices in Switzerland, I saw the energy that Bill was able to generate in his firm through the power of purpose," Polman shared in one of our Conscious Business program sessions. "But when I spoke with Bill, it became clear that before we were able to turn Unilever into a purpose-driven organization, all of our leaders had to become clear about their individual purpose first."

You're a leader, whether by default or by choice. No matter whether you lead a global organization or drive a forklift in the warehouse, you're always the leader of your own life, creating the circumstances of your life, impacting people around you, every day. Once we become clear about our purpose and decide how we want to lead our life even when no one's watching, we discover that in order to bring our purpose powerfully into the world, we don't need to take on the weight of the world and change the existing reality. In fact, we realize the moment we attempt to change something – in business, politics, or education – we create separation, implying that we have the right way and they have the wrong way, ultimately creating conflict and resistance. We're back in the DO – ACCUMULATE – BECOME model.

Our job as authentic leaders isn't to change the status quo. It is to touch and inspire others; to breathe life into a new possibility of how things can be done. That alone has the power to change the world. In Buckminster Fuller's words, "You never change things by fighting the existing reality. To change something, build a new model that makes the existing model obsolete."

As you develop your authentic voice, remember you're not selling anything. Instead, you're offering an alternative pathway to do or look at things. A new possibility that could be of value to the other person. In an organization, it could be expanding performance through building an inspiring culture; for an individual, it might be expanding their mindset and thereby creating healthier relationships with family members; as a sales person, it's offering your customer a new possibility rather than wanting to close the deal. Once we discover the intersection of our purpose and the value it brings to others, we're on track to making a living through expression of our purpose. When you're able to communicate that in a clear manner, people will want to follow you, hire you, or buy what you have to offer – just like Anna, the changemaker from

Chapter 5 who was offered a leadership position because she inspired people with a better way to deal with changes in the team. Her authentic talent and purpose met a real-world need. She created authentic success.

There are several ways in which you can powerfully express what you're in the game for. For our clients, it has worked best to craft a short and powerful statement, which includes three elements: "why you do everything you do" (your purpose or the game you're choosing to play); "how you do it" (stating the environment people can expect when working with you); and "what you deliver" (so that even the most business-focused CEOs perk their ear because there's something in it for them).

Attached to this chapter is a link to example statements and an exercise that will help you develop your own. We've worked with thousands of people on this, helping them access a new level of energy and clarity that moved them into positions and places they had previously only aspired to reach.

Fear: The Inevitable Companion

Every coin has two sides. The moment you expand beyond your comfort zone and speak your truth, you'll be confronted with the inevitable companion of moving into your authentic power: fear. After all, there's a reason why we've shied away from speaking our truth, continued to fit in, or stayed in a job too long: our fear of uncertainty.

As we expand into our potential, whether we identify as man, a woman, Asian or American, we ultimately share the same path: overcoming fear. When we follow our authentic voice (maybe speaking with our boss to build a more inspiring culture, changing our job, or even our profession) our scarcity mindset will be quick to tell us all the things that could go wrong – from losing our job and not making enough money to failing altogether. The Model of Dominance & Subservience awakes once again and confronts us with our previously tucked away fears: we won't make it; we'll be rejected; we'll experience hardship. The journey to authentic success is not an easy one. Not everything will be swell. You'll experience moments of fulfillment, elation, and love, and you'll go through setbacks and times where you need to face the music. But just like going to the gym, over time you become more centered and resilient, able to withstand challenging moments with more grace and inner strength.

Nonetheless, there are a few beacons of light that can guide you in times of fear and uncertainty. First, you'll steadily grow your inner authority and show up from an empowered and independent place, a benefit that will have a positive ripple effect in every area, from career growth to personal relationships. Second, the more you speak to like-minded people about what possibilities you see in the world, the more you'll surround yourself with people who resonate with you, and the more your brain will be able to rewire itself and allow for an alternative reality to emerge.

Ultimately, our authentic journey isn't something that happens out there, in our attempt to change our workplace or eat healthier meals. It is your soul's journey, and every experience – positive and challenging – is a stepping stone on your path.

Help Section: Putting It on the Ground

Even though there's no quick fix for expanding your authentic power in the workplace, there are certain stages and repeating patterns that help along your way. The following five stages are a handrail for expanding your Being in the workplace. They're not meant as a linear progression but as a roadmap, allowing you to zoom out and see the lay of the new land you're exploring.

Awakening

In the first stage of awakening, you become aware of the dysfunctions in the world around you. While others seem content with the status quo, you start seeing the world through a different lens, noticing people and areas of your work that would truly benefit from an upgrade in thinking. You literally enter a different realm of reality from which you're now able to see an entirely new range of possibilities. Since most of the people around you still live, work, and think from within a different realm, they're not yet able to see what you're seeing, nor are they able to follow you where you're going. Their current mindset makes it impossible for you to bring them into your realm of reality. In conversations, they don't understand, give you blank stares, or think that you've smoked too much pot. They respond: "Your idea is great, and it would be nice to do it that way. But how do we make sure that we meet the sales numbers." The more you try to convince people, the more you feel their hesitancy or pushback, which easily leads to a sense of alienation and loneliness.

In stage two of awakening, you're happy to find some people that share your visions and ideas about the world. They show up at a retreat, at a business conference, or at your company. You know that you're not alone anymore. You might even get invited to speak at conferences or company meetings because people notice your different perspective and see that you bring something fresh to the table. Kenneth, a senior HR manager, received the invitation to speak at a Best Workplace conference after his company reached third place. However, he was still hesitant to speak his truth. He wasn't sure how open he could be because he could get rejected or silently ridiculed by the crowd.

This stage is critical because it opens a crack in the system. It provides us with the opportunity to put our toe into the water and speak from our new realm of reality. While we want to open the fire hose, people around us are only ready for sprinkles. During this stage, we find our initial allies, people who don't want us to remain the old person but support us in becoming the person we aspire to be.

Embodying

In stage three, we gain more confidence that showing up authentically actually works. We move from a mental awareness to embodying our authentic voice. We're clearer and more courageous, and our conversations become deeper and more empowered. Our inner drive to change the system so that we can be more fulfilled and happier slowly gets replaced by the desire to make a positive contribution because we've become happier and more fulfilled ourselves. As professionals, we suggest interpersonal activities to our team: personal check-ins or deeper conversations about work, culture, and purpose. For example, Carl, head of diversity and inclusion for an energy corporation, initiated a culture assessment in his team, followed by communication workshops to create deeper, more genuine connections among his people. Susan, director in a large IT company, initiated workshops that were focused entirely on building culture and connection.

The next stage deepens your embodiment. You become more comfortable being yourself at work, and you're willing to face the consequences. The initial fear of "what might happen" has faded to the background because your desire to live authentically is stronger than being safe or fitting in. There's no undo button anymore. You can't go back to business as usual. You're committed to walking your authentic path, even if it would require you to leave your current environment. Along the way, you've found your tribe of people who also operate in a more authentic and truthful way. You've created your authentic voice and are giving your gifts to the world openly. In a way, you feel you're coming home.

At this stage, you start feeling a much higher appreciation for others and who they're here to Be. You love more people, and you love people more. As you grasp the magic of what you've learned, you start translating the wisdom into your leadership – no matter whether you're leading a team or managing the front desk. With your energy and leadership expanding, you create an environment that attracts people who want what you have to offer from your new realm of reality. Your connections deepen and you notice that much of the wanting, proving, and doing from the past fades while your Being expands.

Expanding

Ultimately, in stage five, you're expanding your authentic power in the world. You've created your own environment, inside your existing organization, in another organization that fits your personality better, or in your own practice. People who operate at this stage don't hold back. They speak their truth in an authentic and empowered way, and, because they do, they become the leaders people want to follow. Paul Polman is one example, as he speaks openly about the urgent need to rethink business and his call for business leaders to step up and act courageously.

As we bring our authentic voice into the world, we might not show up perfectly. We're not "there." We won't stop Doing and let life unfold as we bliss out on our meditation pillow. But over time, our Doing becomes an expression of our Being. Instead of pushing ahead to Do something – to move projects along or meet goals – we're pulled to take action by our Being. More and more, we create an environment where our actions become an expression of our inner purpose and convictions – where we roll up our sleeves not because we have to but because we feel inspired. A subtle difference that has the power to change entire workplace cultures. Imagine an entire organization operating from the love of creating a larger impact rather than from fear and control.

To bring our authentic Being into the workplace isn't a stroll in the park. It's a dramatic shift in our life's focus from being safe and accepted to expanding into the uncertainty of whether it is possible to thrive when we're simply being ourselves. That journey is bound to trigger our fears. Therefore, it is good news that this is not our individual journey but our collective one. We all seek to express our authenticity. It's one of our core human needs. Even though you might feel alone at times, know that it is part of our evolutionary journey as humans, with millions of people walking the same path.

On your journey to follow your purpose, you're lucky to be supported by the current changes in our world. We're not living in the 50s anymore. Thank the lord! Businesses must transform to thrive and even survive in the future. As a matter of fact, business is the only institution that will be able to deal with the global challenges ahead of us. Religious and academic institutions aren't changing fast enough; and political institutions are in a gridlock, busy pointing fingers at each other. Business is the only institution that is trained to adapt to new market conditions quickly and independently. Consequently, businesses need individuals that are clear about their purpose, authentic, and empowered enough to lead others into the future.

The previous chapters have been about you: how to expand into your authenticity and how you can bring yourself fully into your relationships and work. There's one more level to address in order to make the new success model work in your life: how can we create entire organizational systems that operate by a new model? We're all part of larger systems, businesses, nonprofit organizations, political parties, or educational systems. Many people speak about the need to transform these larger systems in our society – what's needed is a pathway to get there. How is it possible to create entire organizations where people can be themselves, feel belonging, and join forces to make a bigger contribution in the world? In other words, how can we create organizations with a wow-factor?

Exercise: Develop Your Why-How-What Statement

In the Plan BE Online Course, you'll find a free section titled "Develop Your Positioning Statement," which contains an exercise to help you craft your own statement. You'll also find a document with statements from other purpose-driven individuals. Access the Plan BE Online Course via this link: https://learn.plan-be.us or below QR code.

CHAPTER 10

The New Operating System for Business: Building Organizations that Nobody Wants to Leave

"The current challenges are beyond anyone's expertise. No one in a position of authority – none of us, in fact – has been here before."
– *Harvard Business Review*, 2009

If we want to transform the way we work and conduct business, it's not enough to adopt the new success model for ourselves or become more mindful in our own lives. If our desire is to transform entire systems to become more inspiring, sustainable, and life-giving, we need a systematic approach. We need an approach that can upgrade the culture of entire organizations with thousands or even hundreds of thousands of people, not just change a couple of individuals at a time.

Transforming organizations is a hot topic. What most people are missing, though, is the systematic path to get there. It's clear that the old model isn't working anymore, but so far there aren't many alternative approaches that meet the needs of the existing paradigm for growth and prosperity while fulfilling our deeper human needs for purpose, meaningful connection, and well-being.

In the previous chapters, we covered the steps to expand authentic success in your personal life, your relationships, and your workplace. In this chapter, you'll get a path for building organizational cultures where people can be themselves, feel belonging, and create truly outstanding things. If you're a leader who wants to create that kind of a culture across your team, where the new success model sticks in an entire organization, you need an approach that makes the human side of business – its culture, purpose, and people engagement – measurable, manageable, and scalable.

Where Current Organizational Models Fail

Most of the existing management models and metrics focus on increasing productivity, financial results, or human performance. They're not about building more inspiring or life-giving companies. Only recently, a few human-centered metrics moved into the focus of businesses, such as employee engagement and well-being. But even these people-centric metrics are mostly developed from our current results-oriented paradigm, our DO – ACCUMULATE – BECOME model of success. They are ultimately designed to help companies *do* and *accumulate* more so they can *become* more successful. We increase employee engagement not for the benefit of the employee, but with the expectation of eking out more performance, increasing financial results, or attracting better talent for the organization. If business was a car race, we'd still enter the race with the same car, the same drivers, only with a slightly better tuned engine. In layman terms this is called manipulation, not transformation.

To truly transform the way we work, we must find a balance between people, culture, and performance in an organization. We must apply the new success model to business and make it possible to create places where people are inspired to show up and create new things, knowing deep down that this will ultimately lead to sustainable business performance. The key to a completely new level of business performance requires one fresh thought: the belief that when we place our attention on people, financial performance will follow. If we truly believe that, we're opening the door to another way of business. If we continue focusing on profits first or fall back to focusing on profits when the organization hits a road bump, the organization will remain stuck in the existing way of business.

An example of overly focusing on profits is Apple in 1990 when Gil Amelio took over as CEO. Formerly the CEO of National Semiconductor, Amelio governed Apple in the traditional performance-oriented way: he cut costs, slashed the workforce by one third, discontinued developments of a major new operating system, and implemented new processes. All his measures might have made sense, but they sucked the life out of a mission-driven, albeit somewhat ineffective organization. Apple became just like any other company. During Amelio's leadership, the company's stock slumped to a twelve-year low until Steve Jobs convinced the Apple directors to oust Amelio in a boardroom coup in 1997. Jobs, challenging as he was, believed that if you bring people together to build an amazing product, financial performance will follow.

Bottom line: to transform an organization, we need a framework that helps professionals, managers, and leaders build organizations where individuals feel fulfilled and engaged, where they collaborate instead of competing, which provides an inspiring culture where people want to give their best and deliver positive financial results to top it off.

The New Model for Business

The 4 Quadrant Model, which you'll learn in this chapter, is based on decades of research about how organizations tick, what makes some companies thrive where others fail, why breakdowns in companies occur, and how to fix or avoid them altogether. This model is based on fundamental principles of human behavior, validated with thousands of leaders over a period of twelve years. It is proven to work in organizations from one to 150,000 employees, independent of location and cultural background. But honestly, the last thing I want to do is to convince you that this 4 Quadrant Model could be *the* solution for transforming the way we work. I'd like you to judge for yourself whether this model resonates with you and whether it could make the impact you'd like to see in your organizations.

In our research at the Conscious Business Institute, we discovered that there are five elements (as shown in the graphic) that need to be fulfilled if we want to turn an organization from ordinary to extraordinary.

Graphic 3: The Conscious Business Institute
model for thriving organizations

1. Self Leadership: individuals must be able to "be themselves" and show up in their authentic power.

2. Team Leadership: individuals must be able to experience well-functioning relationships and genuine connections to collaborate effectively.

3. Organizational Leadership & Culture: the organization must have a purpose-driven culture in which people enjoy coming together to make a positive impact.

4. Business Leadership: the organization must be able to have sound processes and financial metrics to ensure financial and environmental sustainability.

5. Conscious Leadership: the organization must develop conscious leaders who are able to maintain a healthy balance of the four previous elements (quadrants).

As we explore the 5 Elements for inspiring organization in more detail, imagine yourself working in an organization that fulfills each of these. Ask yourself along the way: How would I feel if this element was fulfilled in my workplace? Would I leave or would I *want* to stay engaged in that organization?

Quadrant 1: Self Leadership

Imagine working in an organization where you're able to bring your whole self to work: your body, mind, heart, and soul. You're aware of your authentic personality, unique talents, and purpose, and you bring all of these to play in your job. In essence, you can be yourself, and you're being appreciated for being yourself.

People are aware of their individual personality traits and quirks, their out-of-power behaviors, their fears, and they're able to surface these in a safe environment, allowing them to grow in their consciousness. You're able to bridge your inner, spiritual desires with the need to get things done.

The first quadrant fulfills our human need for Self-Expression.

Quadrant 2: Team Leadership

You're able to create well-functioning relationships and genuine connections. People in your organization collaborate rather than compete, take responsibility for their actions, and communicate in an empowered and respectful manner. People feel included and feel psychological safety to fully express themselves, even if their point of view is contrary to their manager's. Connections among peers are so deep and genuine that they even spend vacations together.

Since positive relationships are a key contributor to our overall happiness and well-being, this quadrant fulfills our human need for Connection.

Quadrant 3: Organizational Leadership & Culture

You work in an organization that has a positive, human-centric, and inspiring culture – a work environment where people want to spend time together. This quadrant requires an organization to pursue a higher purpose – a positive contribution to society or the environment. This quadrant makes sure that culture and purpose aren't placed on the chopping block in crisis situations, when losing a big client or when undergoing financial challenges.

Since we all want to be a part of something bigger, this quadrant fulfills our human need for Contribution.

Quadrant 4: Business Leadership

Lastly, we all want to feel safe and financially sustained. This quadrant creates the processes that make organizations run smoothly. It covers the business-related aspects in companies, including financial sustainability, business models, innovation processes, and growth (the traditional business aspects).

Quadrant 4 meets our human need for Safety and Financial Sustainability.

When you picture yourself working in an organization that fulfills each of these 4 Quadrants, would you want to leave or would you beg to stay? We've asked countless people this same question. Unless there's a specific reason – moving to another city or needing to take care of the kids – people choose to stay.

Business is not about business. It's about fulfillment of our deeper human needs. The 4 Quadrants fulfill our core human needs for Self-Expression, Connection, Contribution, Safety, and Growth; and once our core needs are fulfilled, there's little reason to leave.

Unfortunately, in today's business world, most leaders are preprogrammed, even expected, to focus on the fourth quadrant of financial results (unless you're working in a nonprofit, where the focus usually lies on the third quadrant of making an impact). Of course, any forward-thinking organization attempts to address the other three quadrants. They offer leadership development programs, team building events, and they pay consultants to help craft a beautiful mission. But when pressure increases, goals aren't being met, or people's positions are at stake, the Model of Dominance & Subservience takes over our thinking, and our preprogrammed response is to focus on the fourth quadrant. As leaders fall into that trap, their commitment to people, culture, employee well-being or purpose become lip service. They look nice on paper but don't stand the test in daily business. This chronic refocus on profits and margins is the reason why trust breaks down, why people disengage, why the values that are stuck on a marble plate in the lobby never get ingrained into the company's DNA, why entire cultures break.

If you had a leader that told you on Monday how important you are as an employee, that he truly cares about your growth, and wants to create an inspiring culture, then on Wednesday his focus shifts back to financial metrics and company goals. Would you trust that he really cares about you and your well-being? You instinctively know that if he had to make a choice between meeting the company's goals and your well-being, he'd choose the goals. Even though the company might boldly state that it cares about its people, you know that you ultimately need to take care of your own well-being and growth. You're back working in an ego-centric culture. As long as this dynamic prevails, building a truly inspiring organization remains out of reach.

The Fifth Element: Conscious Leadership

This is the reason why the fifth element – the Conscious Leadership circle around the 4 Quadrants – becomes essential if we want to build better workplaces. We need leaders who have both the outer capabilities and the inner capacity to expand the organization in all 4 Quadrants, and keep every quadrant alive and healthy, even when situations get dicey.

California-based outdoor clothing firm Patagonia provides an example of this kind of leadership. In the early 1990s, Patagonia commissioned a study to understand the environmental impact of their clothing materials. After assessing the results of the study, the company's board had to make a tough decision, which could have put the entire company on the line. Patagonia's team had expected that their synthetic, petroleum-based materials (fleece, for example) had the biggest environmental impact. But the study opened their eyes to the environmental impact of their cotton-based products.

To their surprise, they learned that ten percent of all agricultural chemicals in the United States are dumped onto the one percent of agricultural land with cotton. Conventional cotton crops in California alone are dusted with 6.9 million pounds of chemicals every year. With many of the chemicals originally formulated as nerve gas for warfare, health problems followed wherever cotton was grown.

After the study hit home with Patagonia's leadership, a heated discussion started in the boardroom that went on all afternoon. At the time, sportswear made from conventional cotton was 20 percent of Patagonia's business, putting around $20 million in sales at risk. Hardly any certified organic cotton was grown anywhere in the world – not even enough to serve Patagonia's demands. "If we had to hike prices to cover the cost of making clothes from organic cotton, and customers refused to pay higher prices, we could lose our entire sportswear business," Patagonia describes in a case study. As someone put it that afternoon in the board meeting, "With that, Patagonia would be 'toast.'"

The meeting ended when Yvon Chouinard, Patagonia's founder, said: "If we continue to make clothes with conventionally grown cotton – knowing what we know now, we're toast anyway. Let's do it; let's go organic." The board voted that all conventionally grown cotton had to be eliminated from their product line by the spring of 1996.

To make the risky transition work, Patagonia had to help kick-start the organic cotton industry. "We organized busloads of employees, journalists, and representatives from other companies to go to the Central Valley of California to see for themselves the impact of factory farming," the report reads. "In the San Joaquin's cotton fields, for miles around no birds were singing and no insects humming; the air stank, our eyes burned, toxins stained the irrigation ditches. Hired men with shotguns sat in lawn chairs by the "lakes" in order to scare off waterfowl and shorebirds before they landed in the toxic soup."

In the spring of 1996, Patagonia launched their organically grown cotton product line. To their surprise, everything went fine despite charging higher prices. The organic cotton program became a success. Patagonia didn't only survive the transition to organic cotton, the company thrived and created a following of loyal customers. But even more encouraging, the worldwide demand for organic cotton started booming after Patagonia took the first step.

Yvon Chouinard and his board didn't sacrifice the first 3 quadrants when it was time to choose. Rather than securing profits and margins in Quadrant 4, they stayed true to the purpose and values of the organization and genuinely connected with people involved in the transition. They showed up as authentic leaders. In a speech to Google employees, Yvon Chouinard shared, "Whenever we did the 'right thing,' we made money."

Your Pathway for Building Better Workplaces

The 4 Quadrant model enables you to systematically build better organizations and teams – a new operating system for business. It also provides a pathway for you to create a more fulfilling and wholesome life. The 4 Quadrants don't just apply to business. They reflect everything we do. They're based on fulfillment of our core human needs and are therefore applicable to business, personal well-being, creating better educational institutions, and even political systems.

In your relationship with your spouse, for example, I imagine that you want to be able to express yourself authentically (Quadrant 1), you want to connect deeply (Quadrant 2), pursue a common purpose with your partner (e.g., building a house and family) (Quadrant 3), and you seek financial security (Quadrant 4). Even in your personal life, the 4 Quadrants are a litmus test, indicating whether you're likely to walk the streets with a smile or if you feel something is missing.

Or imagine a school where children are encouraged to discover and express their authentic personality (Quadrant 1), where they learn how to build well-functioning relationships (Quadrant 2), are guided to understand the contribution they're here to make (Quadrant 3) and learn the competencies to sustain themselves with what they do (Quadrant 4). How would children feel in that environment, and what kind of adults would this school send into the world?

Conversely, when one of the quadrants suffers, sooner or later we experience a breakdown in that area. We even can see this dynamic in more forward-thinking organizations like Google, which offers every perk on the face of the earth to their employees, from free lunches to waterbeds and big paychecks. Yet when Googlers are pushed too hard to fulfill their goals (Quadrant 4) or can't align with the values of the company anymore, the result is a fallout where people start looking for other options. This was the case with Blake Lemoine, a software engineer who got fired after he started speaking his mind about Google's artificial intelligence technology, LaMDA. If the 4 Quadrants are indeed a systematic approach for improving the way we work and live, let's take a look at what's needed to use this model for ourselves, our careers, and our work.

How to Transform Workplaces

According to McKinsey research, about three out of four transformation projects in organizations fail. When a global semiconductor firm attempted to transform their leadership culture in 2014, 300 of their top leaders gathered for an inspiring conference in San Diego, they underwent thoroughly designed leadership development programs, and then... nothing. The leadership didn't change; the culture didn't change. Even worse, some of the managers just shook their heads and got more disillusioned by yet another initiative that didn't make a lasting difference. One vice president commented on the initiative: "Yet another pig that's getting chased through town."

Many transformation projects fail because they're approached with the traditional business mindset: let's create a linear project with a set timeline and a solid change strategy. But transformation isn't a linear process. Transformation requires a shift in consciousness. It's like being in a tumble dryer; we don't know when we'll be up and when we'll be down. Any transformational breakthrough is difficult to plan or predict, just like we can't predict when we'll get an insight in the shower. But once it occurs, transformation happens in leaps and bounds. Of course, transforming the way we work requires new frameworks and leadership approaches too. When a manager wants to expand a purpose-driven culture across an entire organization, for example, she must have a scalable and replicable process. But new approaches in themselves don't create transformation. Only when people upgrade their consciousness do transformations stick. Once someone sees an airplane for the first time in their life, they cannot unsee what they've seen. There's no undo button for conscious evolution.

To transform our work world, the necessary consciousness shift is from our primary focus on profits and margins (Quadrant 4) as the measuring stick for business to deeply believing that if we nurture Quadrants 1 through 3, financial success will take care of itself. Can we truly believe, not just as a mental concept but with a deep inner knowing, that when we support our people in expanding their authentic power, when we create teams where people truly feel they belong, and when people commit to a common purpose, that positive business results follow? Or do we always keep a back door open, ready to refocus on profits and margins when pressure rises? That's the required shift, which has the power to catapult us from the pressure-driven survival mode to a more expansive, inspiring, and life-giving mode for business.

In the summer of 2018, the Conscious Capitalism Movement hosted their first European conference at the IESE Business School in Barcelona. During the final session, the difference of leaders operating from the "old consciousness" versus the "new consciousness" became painfully obvious. IESE's business school dean was on stage, interviewing four young entrepreneurs, each of them in their early thirties and leading successful organizations between 20 and 150 million Euro in gross revenue. From healthcare to renewable energy, each of their organizations were driven by a purpose to make a positive dent in the world.

As the session unfolded, IESE's dean kept circling back to the same topic, like a broken record: "You're saying that you're building your companies based on a higher purpose, but how do you ensure that your company makes money? A business needs to make money," he insisted.

The audience of 300 cringed, fidgeting with discomfort in their chairs. It was painfully clear that he saw something in front of his eyes that he simply couldn't square with his own experiences and beliefs about how the world works. He could not get his head around the possibility that the entrepreneurs were successful by building their companies focused on purpose, not money. "What do you mean?" they responded to him. "We are making money, we just believe that if we focus on a common purpose and work well together, the money will follow." The dean spoke a different language. Right in front of our eyes it played out that we can only grow to the point where our consciousness has grown. The entrepreneurs on stage were playing in a completely different realm of possibility, which was inaccessible to the dean.

This brings us full circle. Creating a better way to work and live starts with the individual. We can't expect our leaders to go first; it's everyone's job. That's why this book – although it is ultimately about transforming the way we succeed and govern our organizations – starts with you, your authenticity, your gifts and talents, and who you're here to Be.

Although the purpose of this book is to provide you with a richer, more satisfying life experience in your own personal environment, it is also about our evolution as a species. If humanity doesn't expand to a new level of awareness and consciousness, it is clear that we'll continue working and living in the traditional way – stuck in the existing paradigm like the dean at the Conscious Capitalism conference. We'll continue to create more suffering for ourselves, we won't be able to keep up with the rapid global changes, and with our focus on doing and accumulating more, we'll jeopardize the very existence of our species.

What Can You Do

What can you do to make the change you'd like to see, whether you're a manager in a large corporation or a forklift driver in the warehouse? Changing an entire organization can seem too big to take on, and it can certainly be daunting to go out on a limb and speak your truth in an environment that might not be open. Even if you did want to step out and roll up your sleeves, you might not even know where to start. I've thought of Margaret Mead's words many times: "Never doubt that a small group of thoughtful, committed citizens can change the world; indeed, it's the only thing that ever has."

In our era of transformation, we can't expect the impetus for change to come from the top. Many people at the top have reached their position with the traditional ways, and we can't expect top leaders to change what has worked for them. If they're courageous enough to do so, that's wonderful. But for most areas of society, the necessary change must start everywhere: in the middle, at the edges, in startups, from younger generations entering the workforce, and with consumers choosing to vote with their dollars, euros, or Bitcoin.

The first thing any one of us can do, however, is to wake up, become more aware, and shed light on the dysfunctional ways we operate in the world – from the way we work to the way we practice law to what we eat. There's no need to rebel or become righteous. Darkness cannot fight darkness. Only light can do that. As you become more mindful and aware, it's as though you turn on the lights in a dark warehouse. Suddenly, you see all the things around you – the shelves, wood planks, the equipment. Even after the warehouse goes dark again, you still know where things are. When you start showing up more authentically, operating from the new success model and bringing your light and energy into the world, you create a ripple effect in your environment. People who are ready will see the same things you see. And slowly but surely – or maybe in an instant – we witness the world changing around us, in our family, our team, our organization, and the world.

CHAPTER 11

Be the One: Which Path Do You Choose to Take?

"First, they ignore you. Then they laugh at you. Then they fight you. Then you win."
— Anonymous

We're at a crossroads. Our future as humanity will ultimately be determined by the choices we make today. As a reader of this book, it is likely that your soul is calling you to rethink the way we work and live. But to expand into your authentic Being in the real world requires more than words on a piece of paper. It requires embodying our Beingness on a deep level. It requires traveling one of the longest distances we encounter in our life: from our mind to our heart – from a mental understanding of the ideas laid out in this book to a heartfelt embodiment.

You can take all the right steps, use every tool that's given to you, read every book on the face of the earth, but ultimately you can't expand into your authentic power by doing something. You can't *Do* authentic.

It isn't our activism that transforms our world, our organizations, or even our own lives, but an expanded level of consciousness.

When you apply the BE – DO – HAVE success model to your life, you'll find that the journey to authentic success isn't a walk on the beach. You'll go through ups and downs, moments of elation and times of fear, breakdowns and breakthroughs. You *will* fall back into old patterns and get triggered, possibly even daily, simply because we're hardwired and conditioned for centuries to operate from a scarcity mindset with the Model of Dominance & Subservience ready to take over our behaviors at any time. Our mind is programmed to seek security and restore comfort. When you're afraid, your mind immediately seeks to restore the familiar normal. This can mean staying in your job or relationship longer than it is healthy, or checking out and binge-watching your favorite TV show, medicating with food or drugs, or escaping to fun events, parties, and vacations.

Installing the new success model in your life requires a commitment to remain present, even in uncomfortable and uncertain situations. When you're able to do that, you'll find that those challenging situations become the stepping stones for expanding into your authentic power. Any time you feel off-kilter, you can learn in that very situation where you've sacrificed your authenticity, where you've done something you didn't want to do, engaged in a relationship that didn't nurture you, or made a decision that didn't bring you satisfaction. If you miss that opportunity by choosing not to stay present and instead checking out or turning on the TV, there's nothing lost because you'll receive another opportunity to face the music. The learning opportunity will return, usually with a higher emotional load. For example, the first time around you might just feel frustrated about your job, and if you don't use that opportunity to listen to the signals of your soul, the next nudge could be that you feel anger, get a negative review, or possibly even lose your job.

The more you make it a practice to stay present with your fears and challenges, the more you'll see that they become your most precious learning experiences. Your soul will speak to you about what you've come here to learn. This learning will be the most valuable degree you'll earn in your life, because the challenges that you overcome provide you with the inner authority and experience to pass your wisdom on to others. For example, only when you've faced your fear of rejection or running out of money will you have the authority and wisdom to help others with overcoming the same fears.

Inspired Doing

One of the most persistent challenges people share with me is the tension between wanting or needing to create something – to Do – and finding time to Be: to simply be present, enjoy time with family, in nature, or a few moments without to-do lists. "I wonder whether the rat race ever stops," one manager said to me. "My calendar is scheduled three months out, and if I'm not working, my family, the house, or other stuff wants my attention. Of course, I want to spend time with my kids, but I'm so busy that the little time I have with them quickly becomes over-whelming." Everyone's busy, and finding time for creating a life where we're not constantly catching up with external demands seems virtually impossible in today's times.

We've touched on the challenge to act from a more inspired place of Being in Chapter 9. But this issue is so omnipresent that it's worth diving a little deeper. To do and act from a deeper place of being – let's call it inspired doing – isn't simply about working less and carving out more leisure time. Just like suggesting to a chain smoker to simply stop putting a cigarette into his mouth doesn't work, it doesn't work to suggest to a hard-working person to work less. There are deeper drivers pushing us to continue working that we need to take into consideration if we want to achieve success from a more centered and inspired place of Being.

The reason why we're stuck in the existing success model is our deep-rooted fear that if we don't continue to do what needs to get done, we'll fall behind. We're not good enough, we'll fail, get rejected, or lose our livelihood. We all have our own story that holds us firmly in the existing success model. My story is that I won't be good enough, I'll be rejected by people around me, and ultimately end up under the bridge. Of course, on one level, I know that's not going to happen. And yet, my monkey mind still thinks this is a possible outcome. When I'm in this mindset of scarcity, I act from fear – a mindset that makes it impossible to create flow, and therefore impossible to live a truly fulfilling life.

Imagine for a moment that you had all the money and all the time in the world to accomplish whatever you set out to do. Take a breath. You can notice that your mind is able to relax. Your system calms down, and most likely you'd only work when you felt inspired. Everything you don't like to do you can delegate because you have all the money and time in the world. The pressure we create in our lives is largely driven by our worry that we won't have enough money to survive, enough time to get things done, or that we will be rejected by others – all suggesting that we're not enough if we can't make it in this world. Climbing the career ladder can make us successful on the outside, but if this deeper mindset persists, we'll never create the fulfillment, deeper satisfaction, or peace of mind we want.

Eckhart Tolle writes, "We cannot become successful; we can only be successful." No amount of external work or material belongings can fill the void that's created by our fear of not being or having enough. There-fore, what our future holds for us depends on our consciousness. If we keep operating from a consciousness where the DO – ACCUMULATE

– BECOME success model governs our life, no amount of work will get us to a place of inner harmony and well-being. If the seed of our success contains stress and an alienation from who we're here to be, the fruits of our success won't look much different.

To realize inspired doing in your life, to act from a place of inner centeredness and being, requires that the consciousness that drives your actions becomes your primary focus and the actions become the secondary focus.

Aligning with Your Purpose

To act from a more inspired place in the world means that you're not doing for the sake of doing but from a place of enjoyment or purpose. Of course, this isn't always possible. When your toddler starts screaming at night and robs you of yet another good night's sleep, you're probably neither enjoying the situation nor feeling particularly purpose-driven. I'll address those situations at a later stage in this chapter. For now, consider that if you align your life with your purpose (the impact you're called to make in this world) and with your soul's purpose (to expand into your authenticity and be present with every situation that's in front of you), life will start to flow through you.

Picture someone you admire: Mahatma Gandhi, Mother Teresa, Richard Branson, or maybe your postman, and you'll find that – in the situation where you admire them – this person is being fully present, authentic, undeterred in what they're doing. When you're able to align your life and soul purpose, you'll step into another reality where the tentacles of our daily to-do lists lose their grip. You'll bridge heaven and earth, rooted in the present moment, and guided by a higher force – not for your own benefit but to touch and inspire others.

It's difficult to imagine that we can run a business in this way. If you work the production line at General Motors, it seems impossible to work with purpose or to enjoy your work all the time. You can't just walk away every time you don't feel happy or fulfilled and let the assembly line spit out a half-baked car. As a matter of fact, from our existing doing-focused consciousness, it is impossible to create a business where people's work is driven by enjoyment and purpose. It's as if Christopher Columbus suggested to people who thought the earth was flat that they should sail westwards to reach East India. It simply wouldn't make sense.

But once you shift your consciousness and allow your life and soul purpose to align, you'll discover that you become one with life. You synchronize with life itself, and life will happen through you instead of by you. Just like the acorn doesn't harbor ambition to become a tree, you'll be able to shed your ambition to push the agenda or get to the next level. Instead, you become part of life itself, without a doubt that life unfolds for you if you just stay present and in resonance with the universe. You're present with the task in front of you, knowing that it contributes to your higher purpose. Imagine an organization that operates from this level of consciousness where people show up around a common purpose, enjoying what they're contributing to the team in an environment that honors each individual's authentic path, and life itself.

Presence

The present moment is the only place where the fullness of life is found. Unfortunately, our mind always tries to pull us into the future or the past, creating stories about all the things that could go wrong or wonderful images of happiness and success if we just reach the next thing in our lives. And if the future doesn't hold much for us, our mind displays past memories so we can dwell in the good old times.

Our mind isn't comfortable with the present moment. As a matter of fact, to our mind, which in the DO – ACCUMULATE – BECOME success model is largely driven by fear or fantasy, the present moment is the scariest place to be. In the present moment there's no story to dwell on and not much to do other than what's right in front of us. The present moment doesn't care to accumulate, and it never asks what you'll become once you've accumulated everything you wished for. And yet, it's the only place where we can expand into who we're here to be, where we're able to genuinely connect to others or be in synergy with the flow of life.

Only in the present moment, when you're singing in the shower, meandering in nature, or deeply immersed in flow, can you align with the universe and get a glimpse of your own evolutionary trajectory. When you act from the present moment, the consciousness that drives your actions is far more important than what you say or do.

Several years back, one of my advisors stopped me in my tracks when she said: "Peter, nothing is broken, nobody needs you, there's nothing to do. From that place, what do you want to do with your life?" Most of our doing is driven by our impression that the world isn't how it's supposed to be, and therefore we need to fix something, make something happen, or do something meaningful to be relevant. What if that's not true? Our world is a direct reflection of our collective consciousness. From that perspective, nothing is broken. Everything we see around us is a reflection of our global state of consciousness. People abuse their kind because they've experienced trauma in their childhood or didn't receive the help they needed to heal their state of mind. It doesn't excuse the atrocities we see in the world and the pain inflicted on others, but it provides a mirror image of how humanity chooses to live in the world.

Many of us think others need us, but beyond your infant needing you for survival, none of us are really needed on this planet. Mother Earth would be thriving without Homo sapiens. And lastly, most of the things we think we need to do are self-created chores. We spend time and energy building a business, for example, and then it needs ongoing energy to keep it alive.

"Nothing's broken, nobody needs you, there's nothing to do" doesn't imply that our best option would be to open a good bottle of wine and party. These three statements can change your perception because they create space for one question: if this was true, what would you choose to do with your life? An empowering question, because it provides the possibility to show up with no ego, no need to manipulate the outside world to get somewhere, and space to simply be.

These three statements have the power to lift your worry and stress. The moment you live from a place of not wanting and not needing to do something, you're able to respond to what's right in front of you in the present moment. You can even fall in love with what you do, whether it's cleaning the dishes or having an argument with your neighbor. Businesses are created one conversation, one single act at a time. Can you trust that if you show up in the present moment, fully present and able to respond, you'll expand to the next, greater version of yourself? I experienced this magic when building the Conscious Business Institute. Whenever I attempted to grow the Institute in a traditional way, by developing strategies and business plans or infusing my own thoughts of what the Institute should look like, work became a grind and progress stalled. The more I stayed present, sensing the flow of what the Institute wanted to be, the easier it developed. With time, I realized that it wasn't our products that made the difference, but the presence and energy in which they were developed or delivered.

You can only create what you already hold in your consciousness. Of course, you can manifest success by doing more and working harder. But this way of manifestation will perpetuate struggle and suffering. To expand into your authentic power and create from a state of inspiration and enjoyment, Being must precede Doing.

The Three Ways of Inspired Doing

There are three ways to bring inspired doing into the world, three ways which help you act and do from a state of being. When you bring the energy of these ways into everything you do, you'll operate from a higher level of consciousness and increasingly live by the BE – DO – HAVE success model. Any work that doesn't include these three ways activates the traditional success model, usually perpetuating suffering for you or others. You don't need to use all three ways at the same time, and their use will fluctuate over time, according to the situation and the overall state of your life.

The three ways of inspired doing are essence, purpose, and acceptance. Each one of these reflect a level of consciousness that reaches beyond our egoic drive to survive or succeed. Acceptance eliminates our egoic wanting for things to be different. Purpose replaces our egoic need to meet specific goals with our ability to create new possibilities for the benefit of the greater whole. And essence replaces our egoic striving for material outcomes with a way to fulfill our deeper human needs in the present moment. Together, they provide you with the ability to work and live from a higher level of consciousness while meeting the demands of our three-dimensional world.

Essence

Musicians playing a symphony, just like many other artists, scientists, and teachers immersed in their art, aren't trying to reach a destination. "In music, one doesn't make the end of the composition," says the English writer Alan Watts. "If so, the best conductors would be those who played fastest. And there would be composers who only wrote finales. People would go to concerts just to hear one crackling chord." Art becomes an art form because the artist expresses herself in the present moment, without wanting to reach a destination or material outcomes. In the present moment, they experience essence like joy, flow, ease, playfulness, or accomplishment.

In the new success model, essence – the feeling states we seek to experience – replaces the focus on external achievements of the old success model. In a Conscious Business, the fulfillment of our essences becomes the main driver for success instead of striving for more. When the joy for our work, fulfillment from what we create, or deepening connection becomes the focal point of our work, our engagement and quality of life increases. We build a human-centric organization. On the flip side, if our essences such as joy, fulfillment, quality, or connection remain unfulfilled, we disengage. The products we create lose meaning, and the way the organization operates becomes harmful to the well-being of people or the environment.

When you remain in the present moment and experience the essences that drive you, joy flows through you. In those moments, whether you feel connection as you watch a movie with your spouse or freedom when riding your bicycle through a beautiful landscape, there's no sense of scarcity. You are part of life, full-filled by life.

Of course, it's unrealistic to always find joy in what we do. In fact, it's a misconception to hope for a workplace that fulfills your essences at all times. It would be nice, but it's unrealistic. At times, we just need to roll up our sleeves and get stuff done. Our soul didn't sign up for comfort. We signed up for growth. And it's natural that we'll experience situations that challenge or confront us, in which it will be hard or even impossible to feel essences such as joy or peace of mind.

When you search for a workplace where you feel more joy or can express your unique gifts, you might misinterpret how essences work. When you expect external circumstances to deliver the perfect life and fulfillment of your essences, you're right back in the DO – ACCUMULATE – BECOME success model. Your ego is seeking to get to a place of happiness instead of aligning with the flow of life.

It is certainly possible to experience essences through external circumstances. Falling in love with someone can give us connection, and a full bank account can give us peace of mind. Some company cultures will be a better fit for you than others. But you'll find it more powerful to have your essences flow into what you do from deep within you. Rather than finding a job you enjoy, can you bring joy into your current position? When you meet with a client, for example, embody the essences of joy and connection. When you bring these essences into the present moment, your own life experience and your meeting changes.

Essence always originates from a place of abundance. When you show up with an abundance mindset, you break the scarcity thinking that's underlying the existing success model. You become more abundant and bring more abundance into situations. You're only able to give what you have. As you express joy and connection from deep within, you'll create more of it for yourself and the people around you.

Therefore, it is not necessary to find a job where you enjoy every aspect of your work. If you do, all the better. But as a first step, look for a position in which you can express your authentic personality and Magic. Once you've found that, your presence in the moment will bring the job to life. Rather than finding every activity enjoyable, you'll enjoy every activity in which you can be fully present. It's not just the action that gives you fulfillment but the deep sense of aliveness you feel when you're fully present. In this way, even a gruesome task, such as letting someone go, can become a moment of richness, vulnerability, and deep connection as you stay present with the person across from you.

Here's a practice that helps you expand your essences and a sense of aliveness. Scan your daily routine activities that you perform on a regular basis. Make a list of them, including the ones that you don't enjoy doing or find stressful. This can include washing the dishes, doing laundry, commuting to work, cooking dinner, or any other tasks you find tedious. Don't include the ones you detest yet. You can write them on a separate sheet of paper so we can address them at a later point in this chapter.

Pick one of the activities – washing dishes, for example. Whenever you're engaged in that activity, bring an essence of your choice into the activity. Alertness, focus, or maybe even enjoyment or love. Even though you might not actually enjoy washing the dishes, can you bring the essence of joy into that activity and let it flow through you? Make it your emotional gym routine. This way, Being joyful becomes your main focus. You become a vehicle through which a higher level of energy, presence, and consciousness flows into the world.

Purpose

A middle-aged lady is taking care of the public restrooms in the English Garden in Munich. Located right next to the Chinese Tower, one of the most popular beer gardens in Bavaria, her visitors aren't always in the best form when they use her facilities. And yet, when she's on duty, they're greeted with a heartfelt friendliness, enjoy perfectly clean bathrooms to do what they came to do, and even find a bouquet of flowers and nicely placed paper towels on their way out. The lady they meet on their trip to the bathroom embodies the essences of joy, care, even love for her clients. These essences just ooze through her into the world. But she's not just a happy and loving person. She does her job with a purpose. When asked, she'll reveal that the reason she does her job is to touch people with her love and care so that as a result the world will be a better place. That combination of essence and purpose creates Magic, not only in the lives of her visitors, but also for her own wallet. People frequently leave her ten euro notes or even more because they've had a wee experience unlike any they've had before.

Especially when it comes to work, expressing your essence isn't enough to make things happen. Even when you're fully present in the moment and enjoy what you do, people in the business world still want a direction for the company. And you probably enjoy clarity where you're headed in life too. In our traditional success paradigm, we usually use goals to provide that clarity. To be more precise, we use SMART goals, which are specific, measurable, achievable, realistic, and timely. The company leaders set a target to grow revenues by 20 percent within a year; to cut costs by 30 percent; acquire three corporate clients every six months, and so on. And even though we are used to setting and following goals, they leave most of us empty. Constructed by and for the benefit of a few at the top and based on the existing success paradigm, goals aren't designed to fulfill our deeper human needs. Rarely do they encourage people to discover or express their authentic personality.

A goal is a set target that's geared to rally people around a common future outcome. A mental construct, birthed by the egoic mind, to fulfill a desired outcome for the self or a relatively small group of people. There's a desiring inherent in goals, which is usually in opposition to the current state. If a CEO sets a revenue target for the following year, it inherently states that the existing revenue isn't enough. When a leader sets a development goal with her employee to show more accountability, it assumes that their existing behavior isn't good enough.

To succeed in the work world, we need an alternative that can provide us with a clear intention for the future without the pushing or wanting that usually go hand in hand with goal-setting. That alternative is purpose. When purpose originates from the pure energy to create a better future – without the egoic wanting for people or circumstances to change – it combines the essence of enthusiasm with a positive vision to work toward. Rather than opposing the current status quo or pushing people to accomplish, purpose creates a new possibility for the future. It pulls people into joining the movement and releases their emotional energy to make a positive dent in the world.

To an observer, there's an intensity in purpose. But it is different from stress. When you hold your purpose as an inspiring possibility, you can still be present with the task at hand and energized by what you create. Stress is created when you want to arrive at your purpose more than you want to be in the present moment. When you feel stress returning to your life, it is usually an indication that ego has taken the driver's seat. You feel that you're not progressing quickly enough or that things should be different than they are, and so you have to work harder or struggle to get there. You operate from a lower level of consciousness. You pressure or victimize yourself or others, which usually results in emotions such as frustration, anger, anxiety, or blame.

Purpose carries a higher frequency energy. You can see the higher frequency in Martin Luther King Jr.'s "I Have a Dream" speech:

purpose without egoic wanting creates a resonance among people. More than 250,000 people showed up for his speech because they believed in what he believed. When purpose becomes your impetus for creation, you access the creative power of the universe and find that you don't have to do everything by yourself. Many times my clients and I have discovered that once we remain in the present moment, express our essences, and speak our purpose from a place of possibility, we create opportunities without much doing. Doors to incredible people open, clients want to engage with you, and people want to hire you because they sense that you're operating on a higher energy level. What you seek to create is not about you but about a higher purpose that reaches beyond yourself; you're here to genuinely make a positive impact. If the skills match, who wouldn't want to hire that person?

As you shift from the existing success paradigm to the BE – DO – HAVE approach, your job isn't to manage others, to push them, or to get them to do something. Your job is to leave others touched and inspired. To do that, you need to be clear about the higher purpose you're in the game for and speak from that possibility of a better world. When you leave others with an image of what's possible, there's no need to judge the current status quo, no need for confrontation or explanation that things aren't good enough the way they are. As you speak from the possibility of your purpose, you simply provide an alternative reality for others from a mindset of abundance.

Creating a new possibility from an abundance mindset is very different from trying to change things from a scarcity mindset. Offering a new possibility for others doesn't create winners or losers. It includes everyone, even those tough nuts that prefer to hold on to the status quo. The energy of purpose doesn't convince or manipulate. It is the energy of creation itself.

In summary, when you combine the presence of essences such as joy, creativity, ease, or connection with the inspiring and life-giving energy of a purpose, you bridge the heaven and earth elements of inspired doing. You're present in the moment, experiencing the feeling states that enrich your life, while expanding into new possibilities. Both elements are important. Purpose holds a high-intensity energy, which you can't hold in perpetuity. To be powerful and sustainable, the outgoing energy of purpose must be balanced with a core of inner peace that remains intact despite all the external activity. Like the rhythm of your breath, inspired doing requires the inspiration of the inhale and the centering of the exhale.

Acceptance

The third mode of inspired doing is acceptance. It's the approach for the tasks you truly dislike or detest. Very few enjoy going to the dentist or filing taxes. And yet, it's what we have to do. For those situations in which you're unable to create an essence-based experience, let alone find inspiration or detect any meaningful purpose, acceptance can keep you from falling back into pushing or struggling. Acceptance means you recognize this is the situation in front of you; you're required to do this, and so you do it without resisting it. When you file your taxes in a state of acceptance, you're at peace while you do it.

Acceptance isn't a passive state where you just comply and light a scented candle while your inner resistance remains. If you still harbor a grudge, frustration, or resentment, acceptance is a facade. "Beware of the quiet man," the saying goes. If you cover up your inner frustration with a facade of acceptance, you're not taking responsibility for your state of consciousness or the ripple effect it has on the world.

Acceptance requires active surrender. It is an active state of consciousness where you surrender to the flow of life. Through surrender you step back into the energy of the universe. The stress of being here and wanting to be there subsides as you make peace with your life.

When Things Seem to Fall Apart

After I left my career and moved to California, it didn't take long before my excitement waned and I comprehended the possible consequences of my choice. After a few adventurous months, it dawned on me that my move wasn't all purpose and courage and there was a realistic chance for failure. As a matter of fact, during the years that followed, the life I was used to fell apart. First, I realized that the door that provided me the opportunity to go back to my previous life was closing quickly. I had witnessed the dysfunctions of the way we work and live, and I couldn't simply close my eyes, pretend nothing had happened, go back and play by the old rules. It's like noticing in a meeting that the discussion has become meaningless – it becomes really hard to remain engaged with heart and soul.

After that, I realized that I wasn't a venture capitalist anymore. For several years, I had still introduced myself as a former VC, essentially trying to hold on to some form of identity that others would value. On top of that, my marriage had dissolved, and I was living in a house share. My parents stopped asking how things were going because they didn't want to poke more holes into the fragility of my life.

After many layers of my external identity had fallen away, I was left with myself. No fancy job, no big house, no happy family. I remember the day when I received a rejection for a job application that I had submitted a few weeks prior to get back some real-world identity and stability. It felt as though I was left with nothing. In fact, I felt that I *was* nothing.

In the framework of the graphic from Chapter 4, I had left my conditioned personality, and the connections, status symbols, and identities that weren't authentic had fallen away. On my way back to my authenticity, I was left in no-man's-land.

What We Strive Towards

Graphic 4: Life in transition

The path to authenticity doesn't follow the same comfortable and stable rules that most of us are used to. We don't expand into our authentic power by pushing and trying harder. Convincing others of our new path will likely leave us disappointed too because they only know our conditioned personality. They simply can't see the new world that we're seeing. Even more challenging is the fact that we can't plan our path to authenticity. As the inauthentic parts of our life disintegrate, the scaffolding comes off and even the foundation upon which we've built our identity starts to crumble; we won't even be able to plan or explain to others what's next, let alone when we'll be done with the transformation.

Like the transformation from caterpillar to butterfly, our path to authenticity is one of the most breathtaking but also one of the messiest and most uncertain adventures we can take. Friends, colleagues, and family members witness the uncertainty you're going through from the outside. Many will worry and prefer for you to return to who you were before. Meanwhile, you're still vulnerable and not on solid footing yet, so your uncertainty is fed by the worry of others. Our society doesn't encourage people to expand into their authenticity. Most people are tied to the old success model of doing and accumulating. They get terrified when their external world starts to crumble. As someone who chooses to follow the path to authenticity, you become a canvas on which others project their fears. When my parents held their breath after my move to California, they essentially said, "Your decision ignites our fears of not having any status or money." Given that the apple doesn't fall far from the tree, their fear easily resonated with mine.

Life after Death

Death is a doorway to another dimension. Our physical death closes the chapter of our physical existence and makes space for another reality. Likewise, the death of our ego-based, conditioned personality provides a doorway to a spiritual realm that's inaccessible to the ego-based, conditioned mind. When you shed your conditioned personality, it is a natural process to experience discomfort and pain. It is a death of sorts, just like the caterpillar dying in its existing form to emerge as a butterfly.

As you peel off the layers of conditioning and witness your outer world transforming, among all the uncertainty you'll find a new dimension of Being. A space where you feel a sense of aliveness, liberation, gratitude and spiritual connectedness that you weren't able to access previously. Instead of making life's circumstances work for you, you surrender to life. You become part of life. Even in challenging circumstances, when people around you contract and become angry, terrified, or controlling, you'll be able to remain present and centered, like a lighthouse in the ocean, because you see the bigger picture of the events unfolding around you. Some worries will remain, maybe concern about money or losing a client, but you will gradually develop a deeper faith in the unfolding of life.

Rob, who read my colors in the small Carmel cottage, has lived in an alignment with the flow of life from the age of five. While some of his colleagues only feel secure with a client list that extends a few months out, he rarely books his clients more than two weeks out. He's known for more than fifty years now that when he's aligned, clients show up. As a matter of fact, whenever he doesn't want to work, his client pipeline automatically dries up, with flow resuming as soon as his inspiration kicks back in.

When I hit bottom, the nothingness that I felt inside opened a new dimension of life. I met my current wife who, instead of reinforcing my fear of being rejected for being "nothing," told me: "Peter, I don't care whether you bring in the money or not. When you stop living your authenticity, that is when I'll leave. I'm with you." I developed an inner centeredness and a deep sense of feeling guided by a higher force, which gave me more independence from the need for external recognition and validation.

The path to authentic success is a spiritual path, which can unfold in different ways. Some will realize that it is time to leave their existing workplace, some will stay and shift within their organization, and others will undergo a change from the outside, such as a layoff or divorce. Any of these changes can cause pain, but they're part of the journey to authenticity.

The Next Stepping Stone

Many people have asked me what to do in those challenging situations where we feel lost or alone on our path. In those times, know that you're in the right place at the right time. Rather than trying to fix the situation or hoping it will pass soon, create space to simply be – to remain present with the challenge that's right in front of you, to feel your own feelings without the need to do something about it. This is your life. Nobody will give you the space to Be, especially not in our current work world. Instead of asking what you need to do to change the situation, ask yourself what this situation wants you to become aware of. Don't waste the learning; there's a likelihood that you will teach your experience to others at some point in time.

It is your job to stay in resonance with life. If you're here to resonate at C-sharp, do what you need to do to stay in that resonance, even when people around you resonate at B-flat. Find those things that make you fall in love with life again, not from a place of excitement or ego, but from a place of inspiration and love. Get *inspired* by nature, music, art, writing, and genuine relationships so that you don't *expire*. Most of all, remember that you're a spiritual being that's having a human experience. The journey to authentic success isn't just about you. It is our journey together, and, ultimately in a grander scheme, it is an evolutionary journey. Even if you find yourself challenged by life, know that you're here for a purpose, that your journey is part of the evolution of humankind.

We're at the brink of a new age. While the masses still hold on to the existing paradigms, you are one of the individuals ushering in the new age or you would not be reading this book. During the coming decades, every aspect of our world order will be challenged or changed: politics, business, religion, academia, medicine, and what we eat. We will move from the violet age (where people realize the dysfunctions of our world and seek to live with more emotional connectedness and purpose) to the indigo age (where inauthentic ways of living will be challenged and people will seek to operate from a higher level of interconnectedness). This shift is already visible, and every organization will need to rethink the way they operate if they want to attract skilled talent.

In our current state of the world, there's no time to remain a bystander nor can we expect our existing leaders to pave the path. We're called to go first, to be the bridge builders for a new world. Our world needs your creative ability, your authentic expression, and your experience to provide the pathway into a future. In the words of the Hopi elders, "We're the ones we've been waiting for."

RESOURCES

"There's no systems change without personal change."
— Deepak Chopra

Your Journey Ahead

This book has given you a pathway for accessing a higher level of well-being, fulfillment, and wholesome success in your life. Hopefully it has already helped you; however, reading this book alone isn't enough to anchor the new success model in your everyday life. This resources section gives you access to tools that have already helped thousands of professionals create a more fulfilling life. I wish you all the best on your journey ahead.

Access the Plan BE Online Course

The Plan BE Online Course gives you access to chapter exercises, reflections, personality assessments, learning videos, and meditations, which help you apply the principles in this book to your life. Download the meditations, listen to them on your way to work, during a stroll in the park, or when you're sitting in your favorite coffee shop.

Go to https://learn.plan-be.us or scan below QR code to access the free exercises or get the complete course. As an owner of the book, use the coupon code "MYPLANBE" to get the complete Plan BE Online Course for the reader's price of $47.

Join Our Community

Sign up to our global community. Get invited to live calls with the opportunity to deepen your practice and ask questions. Visit www.plan-be. us to join.

Conscious Business Institute
Online Learning Program

Join thousands of changemakers in over 170 countries who have applied the Conscious Business principles to their life, their leadership, and their workplace. Get the most widely used, structured approach for accessing your authentic power, building better teams, creating more inspiring cultures, and becoming a conscious leader. Visit www.cbi.training to learn more.

Conscious Business Master Program

If you're a coach, an entrepreneur, or a leader, or if you're at a moment of transformation in your life where you're ready to take the bull by the horns, apply for this life-changing program. The Conscious Business Master Program gives you an approach and a concrete toolset to bring

Conscious Business into your practice or team. You'll get certified to take the Conscious Business Institute methodologies into the world. You'll even have the option to upgrade your participation to an MA or PhD in Conscious Business. Visit https://master.consciousbusinessinstitute. com to learn more.

Bring the Plan BE Principles to Your Organization

To learn more, contact info@consciousbusinessinstitute.com or call +1 (866) 449-3720.

ACKNOWLEDGMENTS

For their advice, support, and assistance: Mariana Bozesan, Zsuzsanna Ferenczi, Adam Hall, Hazel Henderson, Klemens Höppner, Charlie Kleissner, Joe Laranjeiro, Rod Lathim, Rosalina Macisco, Shawne Mitchell, Tamara Moore, Aileen Panke, Claire Panke, Carlos Sarmiento, Tom Schulz, Bill Sechrest, Mirjam Storim, and Jeanine van Seenus.

I am particularly grateful for my mentors and those individuals who guided me on my journey: Jennie Marlow, Pamala Oslie, Rob Robb and Bill Sechrest, and to my editors Hal Zina Bennett, Katy Koontz, Toni Robino, Doug Wagner, and Carmen Riot Smith for enriching my English with style, grammar, and finesse.

Special thanks to the Best Seller Publishing team for honing the flow of the book, creating the cover work, and bringing the manuscript into the world.

ABOUT THE AUTHOR

Peter Matthies is a former venture capitalist, software entrepreneur, and founder of the Conscious Business Institute (CBI), a global center for transformative approaches for business, leadership, and individual success. Before founding CBI in 2005, Peter served as a principal of a globally leading private equity and venture capital firm, Apax Partners, and for b-business Partners, a $1 billion pan-European VC fund.

During his technology and finance career, he always posed questions such as: How can we establish a more life-giving and sustainable way to work? What are the deep human drivers that shape our decisions, our well-being, and our overall success? How can we build organizations that are financially successful while making a positive impact in the world?

At the Conscious Business Institute, Matthies developed a measurable, scalable, and academically validated methodology for building more inspiring workplaces. More than 60,000 professionals in organizations from one to 150,000 employees have benefitted from the CBI approaches, programs, and online courses.

Peter Matthies is a fellow of the World Business Academy, member of the Evolutionary Leaders Circle, and board member of several organizations.

Matthies is a German native and lives with his wife Rosalina in Santa Barbara, California.